Rainbow of Love

SHORT STORIES

Beatriz Copello

ISBN: 978-81-19654-19-2

First Edition: 2023
Rs. 200/-

Cyberwit.net
HIG 45 Kaushambi Kunj, Kalindipuram
Allahabad - 211011 (U.P.) India
http://www.cyberwit.net
Tel: +(91) 9415091004
E-mail: info@cyberwit.net

Printed at Repro India Limited.

OTHER BOOKS BY BEATRIZ COPELLO

Women, Souls and Shadows, Bemac Publications, Sydney

Meditations at the Edge of a Dream, Glass House Books, Sydney

Under the Gums Long Shade, Bemac Publications, Sydney

Forbidden Steps Under the Wisteria, Abbott Bentley, Pty Ltd., Sydney

A Call to The Stars, (Translated into the Chinese Language), Crown Publishing Company Ltd, Taiwan

Beyond the Moons of August, University of Wollongong, Thesis Collections

Lo Irrevocable del Halcon, Bemac Publications

Renacer in Azul, Cyberwit.Net

Witches Women and Words, Ginninderra Press

No Salami Fairy Bread, Ginninderra Press

Rambles, Ginninderra Press

Contents

THE WOMEN'S POOL

Saturday. Sunny. Summer. Sunny Saturday summer. Perhaps the last hot days of the season. It was a long wait for today after a shit week at school.

Breakfast. A towel, a book , sun glasses and my iPod. Deception and lies. "To the beach with my friends," I have no friends. They wouldn't understand me, I'm different.

The sun still burns, I feel an intense heat on my face. The end of March in Sydney, Coogee. I'm lucky to live so close to the women's pool, just a short walk.

My heart is racing, Oh, I hope so much that she is there. I lie on the rocks. Not many women in the pool today, too early in the morning or shopping. I know most of the regulars. She's one of them. I sit comfortably on the same rock I have sat on every weekend. She'll sit on the grass verge. She'll be here shortly. I put my earphones on and listen to Sinead O'Connor. I'll be seventeen next week.

* * *

I'll be forty five next week. It seems that in the last few months I've aged more than ever. I hate birthdays, especially since I broke up with Denise on the day of my birthday three years ago. Three lonely years since then. My swimmers, my 30+, my book. It's ridiculous. I hate myself for going to the pool just to watch a kid. She must be only sixteen, seventeen, at the most eighteen. If only I had the courage to talk to her. Hail and storms. I wished it was raining to stop my nonsense. Why do I want to see her? I should be at home reading the finance and budget reports for tonight's executive meeting.

* * *

What is it about her that makes me love her the way I do? Infatuation! Yes, mother would say infatuation. I asked her how does it feel to be in love. “At your age infatuations are common,” “Don’t get pregnant whatever you do,” “Love! real love was what I felt for your father,” “One day you’ll meet a nice boy and you’ll love him as I loved your father!” What a lot of shit. Sad news mother ... I’m different. You know I like women.

What if she loves me too? She looks at me as much as I look at her. I wish I had the courage to talk to her. There she is! Her green costume matches the green grass patch. She is looking to see if I am here. Heart palpitations, the doctor said that they are common during adolescence. What about these other palpitations, the ones I feel between my legs every time I think of her.

* * *

She is here. I should wave at her. But if I do she may decide to come and talk to me, and if she comes closer she’ll notice my age. If she knew I was forty five she would not be looking at me. I bet she is short sighted and hasn’t noticed my grey strands of hair. I’d love to caress her all over. How silly of me to fantasize about making love to such a young woman? Tomorrow I’ll make an appointment with the hairdresser and get rid of all my grey hairs. She is reading, an HSC novel perhaps? School certificate books? A Lesbian story? I’ll walk to her and ask her why she keeps staring at me. Oh God, I cannot I’m glued to the ground.

* * *

Maybe my mother didn’t give me enough love, that’s why I like older women. I should talk to the School Counsellor. I dream. I dream of holding her hands. I dream of running my fingers through her grey strands of hair. Today when she leaves I’ll follow her. Her address: a treasure. Hummmm perhaps a love letter under her door. I dream. I dream a beautiful dream: I rest my head on her breast.

* * *

Sagging underarms. Sagging belly. Loose skin. Wrinkles. Sagging breast. I lost my daring spirit. I don't take risks. I'm frightened of changes. My memory is failing. Stress. Cautious about meeting new women. Sitting at home with a book.

There was a spirit who hid in a young woman's body. She liked to have fun. She lived deeply. She loved passionately. She played with the cards on the table. She had ambitions, and plans, and hopes, and faith, and ... What the hell is wrong with me now?

* * *

To be the book that her hands hold. To be the towel where her body rests. To be the hand that covers her skin with suntan lotion. To kiss her. To make love to her. To be her friend. To learn from her. The water will cool my senses!

* * *

Why men have affairs with young girls and no one cares? What would my middle aged friends say if I walked into their houses with a kid hanging from my arm, one who is even younger than my son? I can hear them:

"Cradle snatcher! Cradle snatcher! Cradle snatcher!"

"Look at that old woman with the young girl."

"She probably has money and the kid is with her because of it."

"Maybe she is her daughter."

"In ten years time she'll look like the young woman's grandmother."

"What a ridiculous mismatch."

"Some women near the menopause go a bit funny."

* * *

Tomorrow literature. No "The Well of Loneliness". No "Patience and Sarah". No "Sapho was a Right on Woman". She keeps looking at me. I smile. I feel stupid. Silly smile in a pimpled face. Why would a sophisticated, mature woman like her want to be with me? Pimples. Fat. Insecure. Shy.

"Anorexic," says Mum. "You're too introverted. You need to come out of your shell," says my sister. "Walk straight, you'll get a hunched back," pestered my father before he ran away with his secretary.

Waves breaking against the rock. Fantasies taken away by the seagulls. I murmur my love to the wind: please give her my message. Pain. A pain in my belly. A sweet bitter taste in my mouth.

* * *

I should put an ad in LOTL to meet someone. I have been alone for too long. I'm sick of lonely nights! I'm sick of getting into bed to cuddle my pillow! I'm fed up of the monotony of my hand's well rehearsed movements! A successful life. A successful career. A fat account in the bank. Good clothes. A good car. The opera. The theatre. Lots of friends.

Waves breaking against the rocks. I have a secret. I yearn a young woman and I feel so empty …

* * *

She's getting up. She is leaving.

* * *

She saw me getting ready. She's leaving too. Gosh, maybe when we get to the street we'll say something, but what?

* * *

"Coming back tomorrow?"

* * *

"Sure." Are you?

* * *

"Yeap."

YESTERDAY I WAS FOURTEEDN

I met Georgina the day after my fourteenth birthday. She had moved into the neighbourhood and had enrolled at my school. The morning I noticed her for the first time, she was sitting in a corner of the playground waiting for the bell to go off to get into the classroom. She was by herself, reading a biography of Marilyn Monroe. I don't know why I felt attracted to her because Georgina wasn't good looking. She seemed so lonely, so remote, so out of place in the playground.

When I suggested to my mates, we go and say hello to her, they looked at me with horror. I, Sandy, the most popular girl in school being friendly to a new girl! I never had done that before. I left the group and walked towards Georgina. She didn't notice that I was standing next to her.

"What 're you reading?" I asked. She lifted her head and looked at me directly into my eyes.

"You're Sandy, aren't you? I saw you playing netball. You're a good player! I also saw you in the selffdefence class. I'm not good at sports, but I get top marks in Math". "Math is also my best subject."

"I know."

"How come that you know so much about me?."

"Everyone talks about you."

By the time the bell rang, she had told me a lot about her. Her parents were lecturers at Sydney University, and never had any time for her. She had one heroine in life: Marilyn. She had read every book written about the actress, and her room was decorated with many pictures of the beautiful woman. During the English class, I couldn't keep my eyes from her, it was as if a magnet was controlling my gaze. I studied

Georgina's hair, her back, her legs, every little movement she made. The last period we had different classes, I went to sports, she went to the craft cottage.

Before my sport class had finished, I left and walked to the small bungalow, where the girls did pottery and the boys carpentry. I stood next to a window to observe Georgina Hamilton moulding clay. When the object of my attention came out of class, and saw me standing there like an idiot, her face illuminated with a radiant smile.

"Aren't you supposed to be in sport?

"How do you know?"

"Sandy Durant, I've been at the school for about four months, and I know that you do sports on Tuesdays."

I was surprised to find out that she had been at school for that long and I hadn't noticed her!

Golden autumn leaves were covering the sidewalk. When we left school it was already dark. Georgina and I walked to her place kicking dry leaves and talking non stop. We had so much to share with each other. She asked me in and we had ice cream. Her house was big and luxurious. Many art pieces and strange artifacts from other cultures were displayed on walls and shelves. The Hamiltons, not only had a lot of money, but also had travelled around the world.

"If I was rich, I'd have a house like this one," I blurted out uncovering my deprived background. She looked at me with her blue sad eyes, and explained that a beautiful house didn't mean anything when the people that live in it were all unhappy. Her parents didn't get on. Her father had had an affair with one of his students, the mother had find out, and never forgiven him.

Mr Hamilton was a weak man who didn't have the courage to leave his wife, living terrorized by her menaces. She held on to him by threatening to tell the University Council that he had abused a student.

There was no love between them. Georgina's mother enjoyed the power she had over him and was reluctant to split their assets.

My life story seemed uneventful next to hers, but she seemed interested in me. At school I never talked about my mother, or about my life. Embarrassment was the reason. My mother was a cashier at Woolworths and my father had died at an early age, due to his alcoholic binges. My mother never had remarried or gone out with other men, keeping faithful to the memory of a great man! A great man in her eyes,a pitiful soul in mine. I was determined not to be like either of them.

After leaving Georgina's house, I sauntered home. I took my time as noone was waiting for me. Since my childhood, Autumn had always brought sadness, but suddenly, something had changed in me. The pink and grey sky, the brown dark tree trunks, the bare branches, the golden fallen leaves, and the crisp air, embedded with the memory of Georgina, gave me new and different emotions.

These transported me to a different place and time.

It was as if I was part of a picture on a travel book. I was happy, unusually happy...Dreams of journeys to exotic places, holding hands with Georgina, occupied my mind. Adventures unfolded in my imagination, and in my belly, one hundred butterflies fluttered their wings. Unable to eat anything went to bed with Georgina's image floating in my bedroom.

From that day on, no one at school meant anything to me anymore. I ignored all my so called friends. Girls who were not real friends, but "hangers on". Dummies who felt good by being seen next to the School Captain. Some of them pestered me for a while, trying to find out what was wrong with me. Tania, whom I could say was the closest one to me, sent me letters and brought me presents. She even apologised for things that she may have done to offend me. They couldn't comprehend that all I wanted was to be with Georgina.

I think I started to love Georgina from the moment I saw her. I loved her more than my dog Flipper, and even more than my poor mum. Her long blond hair, her freckles, her little nose and her tiny body became icons in my life. I didn't care that she had pimples, body odour and food got stuck on her braces. My feelings for her had the strength of a hurricane. It was as if a volcano was burning my insides.

Georgina also enjoyed being with me. We had fun every minute that we spent together, whether riding our bikes, cooking pizza or studying. Going to the movies and holding our sweaty hands was the thrill of the week. Walking for hours left us exhausted but exhilarated. We were quite free to do as we pleased. There was no one to stop us. Our parents were busy with their own life. The Hamiltons came home late because their social life was very hectic. My mother worked until very late, doing overtime, stacking tins at the shop.

I wrote poems for Georgina, and she dried flowers for me. She knitted a big blue jumper that I wore until it became thread bare. We swapped clothes and said good night by phone every night. In her living room, in front the big open fireplace, during the long winter afternoons, we roasted marshmallows and read aloud to each other.

Summer came. With sand in our swimming costumes, baby oil on our skins and flies that wouldn't fly away, a pact was made. Never would anyone ever separate us! During those school holidays we learnt to smoke, as well as discovering the meaning of love. One day, after being at the beach all afternoon, we had a shower together. As the cold water ran, we giggled and laughed, lathering each other bodies, trembling, as our hands touched our underdeveloped breasts.

After dinner, we watched a rented video. I was looking forward to sleeping next to Georgina. Her parents were at a function and they were returning home after midnight. Mum had given me permission to stay overnight. She had groaned for hours, but finally had let me stay.

When the movie finished, Georgina suggested to read aloud from a book that she was reading. It was "The Well of Loneliness". We went to bed. I was to sleep in the bed next to Georgina's, but we got together into her bed, and sat leaning against the wall. She read. I listened. When her parents came home, at around three in the morning, we had nearly finished the book. We heard noises downstairs, so very promptly, I jumped into the other bed, and Georgina put the light off. When her mother came in the room, we pretended to be asleep. "They're sleeping." Georgina's mother said.

Until that night, I had not questioned my love for Georgina. But after listening to her that night, I realised that my love was not natural. In the past, I have had crushes with other girls and teachers, but I never had admitted or labelled my feelings. Laying awake, next to Georgina, became a torment as I wanted to tell her how much I loved her rehearsing in my mind my confession, but no words came out of my mouth. I was frightened of what Georgina would say about my feelings. What if our parents found out about what I was? I had given a name to my love ... I went to sleep with a pain in my belly and savouring the word "lesbian".

When we finished reading "The Well of Loneliness" we were sitting in Georgina's garden. When she read the last words, and put the book down, we looked into each others eyes and burst out crying. A few minutes later we were crying into each other's arms. It did not take us long to start kissing with passion. The pain of our love was sweet.

On the way to the movies, Georgina looked worried. She wanted to tell me something but she was embarrassed to talk. After a lot of coercion on my part, she confessed. She was worried because she did not know how we were going to have sex. We needed a dildo, and neither of us would know where to get one, or how to use it. It was a great dilemma. We spent hours at the municipal library looking up in books and encyclopaedias words such as: dildos, lesbians, sex, and dykes. Books did not have the answer.

A few weeks later I had the chance of spending the night with Georgina. As soon as we finished our pizza we went to bed. This time we did not read. We explored our bodies, kissed and touched each other. But that was it! If time had been on our side, we would have learned eventually how to make love.

I was plotting what to tell my mother so she would let me spend the night at Georgina's, when the phone rang. It was Georgina. Sobbing she told me that they were moving overseas. Her father had accepted a position at Oxford University. Georgina had been enrolled in a boarding school in London, and her mother was going digging in Egypt. They had decided to divorce.

In a month they were gone. The last few weeks before they left we hardly saw each other, and then we didn't talk much. An emptiness had very quickly taken over me. She promised to write to me, and when old enough come back to Sydney to be together again. Words said with hastiness and innocence. My heart broke when she left. For a while she wrote to me quite often but then her letters became less and less regular. Finally, I stopped hearing from her. My letters were returned with "unknown at this address" written on the envelopes.

THE FAIRY GODMOTHER

The first and only time I saw her, I had spent three days crying on top of my bed. Three days in which I did not speak to anyone, eat anything or go out. A deep depression engulfed me. All I wanted to do was to disappear for ever. To shrink, to become a zero, like "The Incredible Shrinking Man", a movie I once saw. This man, after being exposed to chemicals, had shrunk, and shrunk until he became a dot in space.

My sorrow was very intense, so intense that I wanted to kill myself to stop the pain. I started to make plans. I considered options like: death by hanging, electrocution, sleeping pills, jumping from The Gap, but I fell asleep in the middle of planning.

I woke up a few hours later. Still aching, I went over in my mind the events that had left me in such a state. In a period of twenty four hours I had lost my job and had a car accident in which the car was "written off". Worst of all, my lover had left me. Not only had he left me but he had told me what he thought of me before leaving. He said I was fat, boring, and insecure. He called me a "dead fish" in bed. As he walked out he screamed: "Frigid!!! Ignorant!!! That's what you are!"

What hurt me more was that he was right. I don't know why he wanted to go out with me. I suspect all he wanted from me was to help him pay all his bills, bills which he finished paying last week. I also provided his meals, accommodation, sex, and did his bloody laundry every week. I knew in my heart that he was going to leave me one day, but I had fallen in love with him. Yes, I wanted to kill myself, to end my miserable life.

From the beginning of my life I have had bad luck. My parents died in an accident. I had no living relatives. I was brought up by a family friend my parents had nominated in their will to look after me. This woman, who is now dead, was mean and nasty, an old fashioned, religious prude. Children at school used to laugh at me because of the way I was dressed.

Meredith was her name. How can anyone leave her child to someone with such a name? Meredith used to force feed me. She fed me so much that I became an obese child, and later, an obese adult. It wasn't as if we had nice food, sweets or delicacies. All she gave me was porridge for all meals. We had porridge for breakfast, porridge for lunch,and porridge for dinner. Once every two weeks she bought me an apple. Sometimes we had mashed potatoes or rice. We had as a ritual one egg a week.

The little money my parents had, went to pay for their funeral and the mortgage on their house, which is now mine. My guardian had money, a lot of it, but she never used it. To get more money she rented her house and we went to live at my parents place.

Dear Meredith made me wear clothes and shoes until they were falling to pieces. I never went to the movies or to the theatre until later in life. Toys or birthday parties were a non-event in my deprived childhood. The witch did not let me read at night because she was afraid that too much electricity was going to be used. School excursions, or practising a sport were out of the question.

We never talked to each other, exchanging only the most necessary words. Grunts and monosyllabic utterances were all that came out of her mouth, except when she preached at me. Meredith believed that an idle person is a sinner. Guess who got up at five in the morning to clean the house before going to school? Even when the house was clean, extra chores were found like weeding the garden, mending clothes, or washing curtains.

Religion was very important in our lives. We prayed at least three times a day in the mornings, in the afternoons and before going to bed.

We went to seven o'clock Mass every Sunday. At home the only books allowed were the Bible and my school books. When she moved to my parents' place, she burned all my parents' books.

The reason why my parents left me with her is a mystery to me. Meredith had been a very good friend of my grandmother. Maybe they thought that she was going to rear me well because of all the money she had, money which she left to the church when she died. The witch's death brought me freedom, but also an incredible insecurity. There I was, age eighteen and ignorant about life or anything else.

After I woke up, I resumed with the plans to kill myself. I was scheming my death when she "PLOPPED" into the room. I should say she popped in the room, but she did not pop she "PLOPPED", because when she appeared in the room, out of nowhere, she made this plopping sound.

"Hi! I'm your fairy godmother" she said smiling at me.

The middle age woman looked like your favourite aunt or a young jazzy grandmother. I always had imagined fairy godmothers dressed in pink organdie frilly dresses. The fairy godmother, my fairy godmother, was wearing jeans, boots and a bright and colourful shirt, with a scarf around her neck. She was holding her wand which reflected a multi-coloured light when she moved her hands as she talked. She floated easily on top of my bed, as I was pinching myself to make up my mind as to whether I was sleeping or awake.

"Stop that nonsense", she ordered.

"Who did you say you were?"

"I said I was your fairy godmother. I've come to help you. But don't expect me just to move my wand and make it all sweet and lovely for you."

"Oh!", I exclaimed in wonder.

"I know that you've had a rough time, that's why I'm here. I like my goddaughters to achieve their success on their own. Some of my darlings don't need any help, but you...! I'll give you advice and I expect you to succeed! I want you to become a strong, successful and happy woman."

"What will happen if I fail?" I asked in a trembling voice, still not convinced that I wasn't dreaming.

"Well if you fail you'd better kill yourself!", she said in a not very friendly way.

"O'K, here you are!", the godmother said waving her magic wand.

As she moved the wand, words, as if written with lipstick, appeared on the mirror of my dressing table. Once the message was completed she pointed the wand at me and added: "Remember, this is your only chance. Don't blow it!" Then as she arrived she left. The fairy godmother plopped out of the room, leaving behind a pink and yellow cloud studded with gold sparks. A cloud that disappeared a few seconds later.

I was about to get up and read the message when the phone rang. I answered. It was my ex*f*boss to tell me that I could have my job back if I wanted it. He said that he wasn't able to replace me. Still in shock because of what had just happened, I told him where he could stick his miserable job. I figured that if a fairy godmother was prepared to give me a go, I mustn't be the "shit" I thought I was. From my bed, I was rereading the instructions when the telephone rang again. I answered.

"Hello."

"Hi, how're you?"

"Better. Thanks."

"The prick is about to ring you. He wants you back. Can you believe it. The arse hole!"

"I know."

"What do you mean you know?"

"He rang me already. I told him where he could stuff his bloody job."

"You didn't."

"Yes, I've done it. I've been wanting to do it for long time."

"I've got to go. He's watching me."

"Hang on. Do you know anything about fairy godmothers?"

"You mean gays?"

"No! Not that sort of fairies! Fairy godmothers?"

"Have you flipped love? You've been inside too long. I'll come to see you after work."

"Don't worry. I'm fine. I was just kidding. I'll ring you soon."

Finally, I got close to the instructions. It took me a long time to understand them. She had appalling writing! All she said was:

"SEARCH FOR YOUR HAPPINESS WHERE THE GODDESSES HAVE HIDDEN THEIR

TREASURE. LOVE THE CONVEX, BUT LOVE MORE THE IMAGE IN THE MIRROR"

After reading the message a great disappointment overcame me. I didn't understand a word she had written. Although disappointed, I was prepared to do anything to understand the meaning of her message. Surprisingly enough, I was no longer depressed. I was feeling really great. It was around four o'clock when I decided to go to the local library seeking the interpretation of her words.

My first question to the librarian was where could I find any books on fairy godmothers. She pointed to the children's section. After a few minutes trying to explain what I really wanted I gave up and went home. The message on the mirror had disappeared. Luckily I had copied it down. I was looking at the mirror trying to see any vestiges of the writing when I saw my reflection.

Previously I had avoided mirrors at all cost because I hated myself. I hated my fat and sagging body. "Love more the image in the mirror" the message read. Maybe that was what it meant I should love myself. But how could I love myself if I didn't even like myself. I spent most of the evening trying to figure out the message.

The next day I was back at the library. This time I was luckier. When I asked the librarian for books on selfƒlove she understood me. Hurrah! She kindly said that perhaps I was talking about selfƒesteem. I agreed because I was embarrassed to admit that I didn't know what she was talking about. I borrowed the four books that she took from a shelf.

Once at home I read, and read and read. The more I read the more exhilarated I became. The fairy godmother was right, I had to like myself and love myself. In an unusual gesture of selfƒlove, there and then I decided to look after my body. No more booze, cigarettes or junk food! I also decided to join a gym. I had some money saved so I didn't need to go looking for a job yet. Besides I was a different person now: I wanted a job that suited me! I didn't know yet what sort of a job, but I was sure I was going to find one.

The days went by quickly and the muscles in my body started to show. I was happy. Every free minute of the day, after my aerobic, weight lifting and self defence classes, I spent it at

the library trying to find out what the rest of the message meant. I read books from the history section, from the philosophy shelves. Mythology and theosophy fed my brain.

Spending so much time reading, I developed an interest in books and studying. In no time, I had enrolled at the university. I was lucky that my guardian had allowed me to finish high school. I was a good student, easily passing subject after subject. These successes made me feel better and better about myself. I was happy with my life and with myself although I still didn't fully comprehend my fairy godmother's message.

...and then she made her triumphal entry into my life.

It was a grey autumn afternoon. I had to complete an assignment and decided to go to work in the library. I had spent a few hours there but I hadn't written a word. A younger woman at a nearby table kept staring at me. The funny thing was that I kept staring back at her. As the mutual staring became more intense, I became more anxious about not being able to finish my work.

Why not ask her why she was looking at me? I decided to ask her for a coffee instead. She accepted. That day we got caffeine poisoning. The two of us spent the rest of the day drinking coffee and talking about each other. Before going home, I asked for an extension to hand in my essay late. Holding hands and kicking the golden leaves that lay on the ground, we walked to my place. That night I made a few great discoveries.

I wasn't frigid after all! Natalie knew about women and how to love them. It was so easy for me to love her back. After a few weeks of running between the university and her bed or mine, my sexuality, my past frustration, my failed relationships, everything fitted into one simple word : LESBIAN, I was a lesbian.

By the time I realised I was a lesbian, I also realised that when the fairy godmother said "Love the convex" she meant love women. How did I figure this out? Very simply. I was in a Psychology class when the lecturer, talking about Freud and the symbols of the subconscious, said that in Freud's eyes anything round, circular, or convex stood for the female genitalia. Eureka! My Godmother knew I was a lesbian. and I'm sure she is a Lacanian Feminist. I was thrilled to have decoded half of the message!

I was in my last year of psychology when, by chance I came across the meaning of the rest of my fairy godmother's message. "Search your happiness where the Goddesses have hidden their treasure". Now that I know what it means it makes sense. Without realising it, and in my search for solving the puzzle, I had done exactly what she had said in a very obscure way: study and use your mind. I never saw my fairy godmother again, but I'm sure I haven't disappointed her.

I found the answer in an old book with legends. The Goddesses had a treasure: KNOWLEDGE, but they didn't want to give it away to humans, because things that come easily are not appreciated. They discussed the problem and decided to hide it those who found it could keep the treasure. But they didn't know where they could hide it.

"Why don't we hide the treasure at the bottom of the sea?", asked one.

"No, let's hide it underneath a mountain", said another.

"I know of a better place, let's take the treasure to another planet", said one of the oldest goddesses. When one of the most intelligent goddesses, who only spoke when she had something worth saying, said:

"The best place to hide the treasure is within their own minds. If they find it, they can keep it." And so it happened that the Goddesses hid their treasure inside the mind of human beings.

THE NEW NEIGHBOURS

Please note, no racial offence has been intended with this story. It has been written in a spirit of fun!

I always thought that people who wrote to magazines asking for advice were idiots, but I've changed my mind. I'm in trouble and need advice. I honestly don't know what to do! I must make a move quickly otherwise I'll be in real hot water. Perhaps my life is in danger, who knows? These people are weird! I'm seriously considering ringing someone: but who? Cleo Magazine? Woman's Weekly? I'll have to phone because if I write when the reply arrives it may be to late.

It all started only a few weeks ago. In fact it was when the new neighbours moved into the house next door. I watched them through one of the front windows as they carried in boxes and boxes. Not very long after I got to know them all, one by one, Signora Pierina, the mother, Signore Rigo the father,Pino the son and Concetta the daughter in law. When the house went up for sale I was hoping secretly that some dyke would buy it since Leichhardt has now become Dykechhardt, but no such luck!

The following Sunday after taking the dogs for a walk, I sat to watch a bit of television. I was so engrossed in this program about dolphins that I didn't hear the bell ring. Suddenly, this terrible thumping at the door brought me back to reality. It was Signora Pierina. "Ciao cara! Me Signora Pierina, new neighbour. Me make cake every Sunday, but no plenty flour! Love gimme cuppa flour pliss. What's your name love?"

I had no time to answer because she left me with the words in my mouth. She pushed me, walked in and installed herself in my living room. I gave her a mean look to let her know that I didn't like what she was doing. No effect! She sat there holding the cup, resting her hands on her apronned lap. After an hour and a half, I knew all about her life, about the life of her family and about nearly everyone she knew back there, in the little village where she'd been born.

Signora Pierina finally left. I was exhausted after such a long one way conversation in broken English. You may wonder why I didn't kick her out. Well I believe in Multiculturalism and all that jazz, so I figured that if I asked her to leave I wasn't going to be very "multi" was I? Anyhow, she left with the cup of flour in her hand not before kissing me on both my cheeks, leaving an itchy feeling just where she'd rested a huge hairy mole that she has on her upper lip. After cursing my luck, I promised myself I wasn't going to open the front door without first checking who the caller was.

Two days later, as I was getting ready to have my dinner, again: THUMP! THUMP! THUMP! at the door. I looked through the peep hole and when I saw what I saw a shiver went all the way down my spine. A beautiful creature of the female sex was standing at my front door. She was wearing a mini and a very tight top which showed her curvaceous shape. I realised that she was one of the new neighbours but without any hesitation or delay I opened the door and smiled at her. "Hi love! Can I use your phone? Ours is not connected yet" , she sing*f*songed. Her voice was melody to my ears! Without saying anything I showed her into the kitchen where the telephone was and where my dinner was getting cold. She noticed my plate of vegies and said pushing me into the chair, "Eat dear,eat please I don't want to bother you" . She sat on the edge of the telephone table, swinging her long and black stockinged legs. As she waited for someone to answer at the other end, she took a packet of cigarettes out of her pocket and lit one. "NO! NO! NO! NOONE SMOKES IN THIS HOUSE" screamed in my thoughts, but not a word came out of my mouth.

I sat there watching her and listening to her raving in her lingo. She spoke for what seamed hours. During this time, I played with my mashed potatoes, my carrots and my peas. I was so taken by her that I couldn't. She knew I was watching her because from time to time she smiled at me. When she finished the conversation, I showed her out. As she was getting out and while I was holding the door open, her body brushed against mine. I sighed. She sighed too!

I've always been an independent dyke. I like to do my own repairs around the house and to my car. I also do any heavy job like painting or mowing the lawn. So far I've survived without the help of any man. Sometimes my dad wants to come and do things for me and I tell him off. You'll understand why I'm telling you this when I explain what happened the Sunday after Concetta came to use the phone. I was mowing the front lawn, enjoying the sun and the exercise when the old man, Signore Rigo, jumped the small fence dividing our properties, pushed me aside and took over my mower.

After the initial shock, I explained that I really appreciated his consideration but didn't need his help. He either didn't hear or didn't understand me because he kept saying: "Nice day, nice day." Desperately I tried to communicate with him. "Comprende me lawn mow, me mow, me mow", I screamed at him. I think he got a bit of the message because he said: "Woman no cut grass, woman no strong, man plenty strong, man cut grass for nice signorina."

"Shit", I said and pushed him aside. He pushed me back. I pushed him back. He pushed me again. Finally I walked away. I sat in the living room wondering what to do. I thought of calling the police, an interpreter, the community justice centre, an italian friend I had in primary school, but I discarded every possibility. I couldn't figure out what to do. Most neighbours have always ignored me. Usually they don't want anything to do with me, for them I'm too..too...well never mind.

"Finitto, finitto, finish!, the old man said as he walked into the house. In my despair I'd left the front door open!

"All done, pretty, very pretty grass", he said with a gloating smile. "Thanks for nothing", I murmured between my teeth. As I got up to push him out of the house, he grabbed one of my arms and feeling it said: “Strong woman signorina. Oh!!! I like strong woman! He mumbled salivating between the gaps of his teeth. I moved away disgusted, showing my revulsion on my face. He came closer. Yuk! I was about to punch him when Signora Pierina walked in the house. Very quickly he moved away and with a serious expression on his face he left.

Signora Pierina kissed me muack! muack! one on each cheek.

“Good dinna for you. You too skinny, plenty food for you”, she said as she pushed a plate full of cutlets into my hands. All of this happened in a split second. When I realised what she’d left me, I ran after her to return the plate. “I’m a vego, I’m a vego”, I kept screaming behind her. “Bye*f*bye”, she said as she slammed the door on my nose. The dogs loved the cutlets.

Two weeks had passed since the lawn and cutlets incident. I was anxious about encountering one of the new neighbours. Again I was virtually a prisoner in my own house. During this time the door bell had rung a couple of times but I’d ignored the calls I didn’t even looked through the peep hole. I had all my blinds down and hadn’t been out to the front or back yard. I had taken the dogs for walks at 4 a.m. Sick of this situation I decided it was ridiculous to hide myself. I was going to go back to my normal activities and if they interfered with me I was going to do something drastic. After my decision I felt really good. It was a nice sunny day with not much wind. Ideal weather to paint the outside guttering. I gathered all the necessary tools and pots of paints plus the ladder and dragged everything to the front yard. I was being very quiet in order not to attract any attention.

So far so good! I’d painted without any problem for quite a long time. It must have been lunch time because I was feeling hungry. Suddenly, the ladder started to shake. In panic I looked down to see what was happening. It was one of the neighbours. Pino, a giant block with a silly gigolo moustache was shaking the ladder. “Stop it! Stop it!

you fool! I screamed with indignation as the bastard pulled me down holding onto my tits. "What're you doing mate?," I kept repeating.

"No paint, me paint. Nice woman relax. Pino paint for nice lady", he said.

"Fuck you mate! Who do you think you are? This is my house and I paint all I want!" I screamed as I pushed him.

"Me paint! Me paint!" he kept saying waving the brush.

"OK you fucking paint all you want I'm going to call the police to get you out of here", I said walking into the house.

"Fucking, lady said fucking?" he said when he caught up with me in the hallway. He pushed me against the wall saying:

"Nice lady need Pino", he said in a romantic voice trying to kiss me.

"I don't need any bloody man", I shouted as I thumped him one with my right hand in the left eye kneeing him in the balls. He got the message. Bent in two he left mumbling something in his lingo. That weekend I finished the painting.

A few days had passed and the neighbours hadn't shown up.

I was relieved as I thought that finally they'd understood that I wanted to be left alone, and that I didn't need any help. Then one night at around 8 p.m., when I was watching a good program on the telly with my feet up and a beer in my hand a knock at the door disturbed my bliss. Yeeees the neighbours were at the door! I had forgotten about them. This time Signora Pierina and Concetta were standing at the front door. They both were shouting at the same time. With panic reflected on their faces and their arms waving around they were trying to tell me something. I couldn't understand what they were saying so with my loudest voice I shouted back: "Shut up you dingbats!" They got such a shock that they did shut up. "O.K. Now only one of you tell me what do you want?" I said modulating every word.

Concetta explained that the men were out hunting ducks and they weren't coming back until the next night. Meantime in their kitchen there was a gigantic spider, which was about to jump on them. They both were frightened and they wanted me to kill it. Stupid me, I felt sorry for them so I went to see the terrifying arachnid. Also I thought that if I didn't go they may have sat with me until their husbands returned. Once in their house, they led me to it. On one of the walls rested a harmless little spider. Overwhelmed by cheers from the two women I took a tissue from my pocket and gently picked it up. "Kill it! Kill it", both women shouted in unison. "Don't be silly women. It's only a harmless spider and it has the right to live just as you and I do", I said as I walked out and ran back home concerned they may have followed me.

Back home I relaxed to watch the late movie, it was Friday and I had no other plans. About an hour later, more thumping at the door. What now? I wondered. It was too late to be any of my mates. Was it the neighbours again? I checked through the peep hole. Concetta with a bottle of wine was standing at the front door. She knew I was watching her because she smiled and said: " Please open! It's me, Concetta", she begged. I opened the door and she walked in. She wanted to celebrate my act of bravery so she had brought a bottle of Chianti. I couldn't refuse. I'm human after all. I led her in and showed her to a seat. I sat on the double sofa. I opened the Chianti and poured it in to my best glasses I also put some soft music on the C.D. player.

It was easy to talk to Concetta. Sshe was bold and sincere. She told me about her problems with her husband, the idiot with the gigolo mustache. She also had problems with her in*f*laws. Concetta felt like a prisoner because she was not allowed to do anything on her own. She complained that she didn't even enjoy sex. All Pino wanted was to satisfy his own desires. The charming woman was waiting for the right opportunity to take off.

We finished the Chianti and continued with the wine cask I had in the fridge. She was now sitting next to me and we were looking into each other's eyes. I noticed that she was breathing heavily. Suddenly we were rolling on the floor kissing passionately. What fire! What passion! Sparks darted out of our bodies. I asked her if she minded making love to a woman. She confessed that she had done it before. Back in her village, she had a good friend with whom she did this sort of play. "Let's play!", I said nibbling one of her ears.

After a glorious night of love making, Concetta got up and kissed my forehead. "I love you", she murmured as she left. I spent the rest of the weekend thinking about her and hoping for her return, but she didn't show up.

Five days had passed since that night in which I'd tasted Mediterranean ardour. I had not seen or heard Concetta. I wanted to see her, to make love to her again, to smell her sweet perfume, to hold her in my arms. This morning I was getting into my car to go to work when Concetta appeared out of thin air and gestured to me to open the passenger door. She jumped in and pleaded: "Drive! Drive as fast as you can!" With tears in her eyes, she told me she'd an argument with Pino. He wanted to make love to her but she refused. He called her frigid so she retaliated by replying that she was only frigid with him. With blind fury Pino had demanded to know with whom she wasn't frigid. She didn't want to tell him, but he twisted her arm so she spilled the beans. She told him! FUCK! FUCK! ...AND DOUBLE FUCK! "I'm running away with you darling", she said.

Concetta at this moment is sitting in my office, in the parking station where I work. She has been sitting there since we arrived at 9 a.m. It is now 5 p.m. My workmates have walked in and out all day, but nobody has asked me about Concetta. I acted as if she wasn't there and she just sits there and smiles at me every time I raise my head.

THE MODEL

Finally Rhoda had saved enough money to pay for a model to pose for her. She had found it very difficult to draw the female body from her own imagination or even from photographs or pornographic magazines. Rhoda felt that the human contact, the relationship between the artist and the model, was necessary for an evocative creation, she believed that this relationship was reflected on the canvas. Rhoda explained this phenomenon to her students as a passage of energy, an energy which was produced and transmitted by one human being to another and from there to the canvas.

Rhoda felt exhilarated. The last time that she had felt like this was when she had broken off the relationship with Peggy. This relationship had dragged her into inanity, inertia and instability. The three terrible "I'S"that had stuntedher creativity. Having to wait for the model gave Rhoda the chance to relax away from her pencils, oils, charcoal, turpentine and brushes. In the last few months, she had not allowed herself a minute of rest. She had been working non stop. It was as if she wanted to regain all the time she had lost while living with Peggy. Rhoda sat in the tiny courtyard at the back of her worker's cottage in Newtown. With her eyes closed, she let her thoughts wander while enjoying the warm but pale winter sun.

Finally it was four o'clock. The model was about to arrive. Rhoda went back into the house and as she walked towards her studio she felt dizzy, realising then that during the last two days she had not eaten much. During this time she had been working on a series of charcoal drawings. She had been so eager to finish them that she hadn't eaten anything in order not to interrupt her work. She went to the kitchen, opened the food cupboard and the fridge but she couldn't find anything edible. All she had was cat food and mouldy cheese. Just as she thought she should go shopping she heard the much awaited knock at the door.

Rhoda opened the door to find in front of her the most unusual woman that she had ever encountered. Her features, her eyes, her body, even her clothes were different. She stood in front of the model without saying anything. Sshe was absorbed by the strange beauty of this woman. The woman was short, very short. She was plump but not terribly overweight. She had long hair, very tight ringlets that fell in masses over her shoulders and her back. Her eyes could hardly be seen as they were hidden behind her curly fringe. She was dressed in what could be called a gypsy or a hippie look. Rhoda was studying the model's body when her voice brought her to reality.

"I haven't eaten. I don't know if I will be able to sit still for too long. When I am hungry, I become very restless and moody", the model said raising her eyebrows in an expression that made her look frightened.

"Well what a coincidence. I'm hungry myself. Come in. Please make yourself comfortable while I go to the deli to get us something to eat. By the way my name is Rhoda", said the painter, thinking how lucky she was to get a model that she really liked. Yes, Rhoda liked the model very much!

Rhoda and the model ate as if the meal was their last, and not a word was exchanged as they ate. In no time they devoured the vegetable pies and salad that Rhoda had bought in King street. Angela, the model, told the artist that she had just finished with her boyfriend because he was a first class pig. He had kicked her out of their rented house without any clothes or money. He wanted her to sell "fits". She refused so he got angry. Rhoda wasn't very keen on listening to Angela's problems. She was anxious to start the drawing session. It was hard to interrupt Angela, she spoke non stop. Finally, loosing her patience, Rhoda got up and gestured to Angela to follow her into the studio. Once in there she told the model to undress, indicating to her which position to adopt.

Drawing Angela gave Rhoda a sensuous pleasure. It was as if each part of the body she drew become part of her. Angela's black eyes, her black hair, her lips, her smile were now all hers. Angela's body was trapped not only on the canvas but also in Rhoda's mind and soul. It was a primitive feeling, even an evil feeling which frightened her. Rhoda thought that owning someone's soul was not very nice. Rhoda smiled at her silly thoughts, thinking "Nevertheless she is mine."

Absorbed in her thoughts, Rhoda didn't realise that Angela was weeping. After a few minutes, Rhoda became conscious of the unusual noises that she was making. Rhoda ignored her because she didn't want to stop her work. She had already lost a lot of time. Another few minutes passed. Now Angela's sobs made her whole body shake. It was a wild cry, full of sorrow and pain. Rhoda could no longer ignore her and asked what was wrong.

"I'm pregnant. I don't want a child from that prick. I don't have any money or anywhere to stay", she said sobbing between each word, concluding her speech with a bellowing sound. Rhoda went close to Angela and held her in her arms.

"Calm down, calm down", she kept repeating. She couldn't think of anything else to say. She never had been very good with words. That had been her problem in all her past relationships. Some of her lovers had accused her of being cold, insensitive and keeping her feelings to herself. Rhoda believed that all of them were wrong. She had loved, she had desired, she had enjoyed, she had suffered. Rhoda's problem was her inability to express her feelings. She could only express her feelings through art.

After a while, Angela stopped crying. Her eyes were close. She had fallen asleep. Rhoda let Angela's body rest on the cushions were she had been posing. She mentally cursed her luck but, despite the anger, she picked a blanket from her bed and placed it gently on the model. She decided to go for a walk. She needed the fresh air. The night was cool. The fresh air hit her face. It gave her a pleasant and invigorating feeling. Newtown was full of people. Many shops were open and the restaurants and cafes were packed. Rhoda loved walking in King Street at night. Invariably she either met dykes she knew or spotted other lesbians walking hand in hand. This made Rhoda feel good. It allowed her to feel that she was not an isolated human being, but part of a community where many others were like her. Rhoda stopped at a gay bookshop to pick up the latest issue "Lesbians on the Loose". She browsed around for a while and then went for a coffee across the road. She sat, with her cappucino, watching people and assessing them in terms of whether they would make good subjects or not. It was around midnight when she returned home. Angela was still sleeping. She sat next to her and watched her sleep. Rhoda had to control herself as she desperately wanted to kiss Angela.

Rhoda woke a few times during the night. She had the feeling that something was going to go wrong. At seven o'clock she got up as she did every Thursday, the day on which she taught at East Sydney Tech. She showered and dressed very quietly in order not to wake up Angela. She left wondering whether she should have told the model to leave. She was a stranger. Someone who knew someone, who knew someone, who knew that she needed a model. Telling her to go was probably the most sensible thing to do but as a feminist, she felt she had the moral obligation of helping other women.

Rhoda loved teaching, but that morning she was unable to get involved in her class. Sher mind was back at the house. What if Angela walked out with her C.D.s, or with her valuable paintings? Perhaps she preferred the few pieces of jewelry that her mother had left her and that she never wore? She should have woken Angela, paid her, and told her to go, but she didn't and now that worried her. Rhoda's students were surprised to see her leave the class so early. Usually she stayed behind to answer questions and to talk about any concern they might have.

When she arrived at home, Rhoda could hear music coming from the house. The music was so loud that Angela didn't hear her walking in. Angela was lying on the studio cushions reading a book. Rhoda walked to the C.D. and pressed the stop button. Only then did Angela realised that Rhoda was home. She jumped to her feet and hugged Rhoda. Rhoda was shocked by her impulsiveness and all she could do was smile. Angela took Rhoda's hand and said:

"Come to the kitchen with me. I have a surprise for you! I borrowed some money from a friend and bought some food. Ar'you hungry? Look spaghetti!" she exclaimed lifting the lid off the pot. Rhoda didn't know what to say and decided just to let things happen.

During lunch Angela didn't stop talking and Rhoda loved hearing her. Angela's face was so expressive! So exotic! So unusual! She was beautiful and very entertaining. During lunch the conversation moved to the topic of lovers. Angela asked Rhoda if she had a man. Rhoda told Angela that she was a lesbian. Angela didn't comment and continued talking and firing questions. By the end of lunch Angela had Rhoda agree to allow her to stay until she could find a place to live, and to arrange for her to have an abortion. Angela had the power to get answers from her without allowing Rhoda to use her logical and rational mind.

Since the abortion Angela had slept non stop for three days. Rhoda had not been able to work as the model was sleeping in the study. Rhoda was furious with herself for allowing this situation to arise and decided to tell Angela to start looking for a place to live. That afternoon she told her.

"If tomorrow you're feeling well, you should go and look for a place to live."

"Oh Rhoda!" Angela exclaimed arching her thin eyebrows."I thought you were my friend. I've noone in this world. I've nowhere to go. Please let me stay until I save some money. I'll do anything you want me to do. I'll pose for you and I won't charge you", she begged as she hugged Rhoda placing her head against the artist's chest.

Rhoda trembled as she felt the young woman's body against her. Rhoda had been without sex since Peggy. Angela's big bust, her hair brushing her chin, her little belly pressed against her all became a torment.

Rhoda took a few deep breaths in order to regain control of the situation. Angela's body had stirred up sensations that had been asleep for a while. "All right, you can stay here for a week. Only one and that's it!". Angela stood on her toes to reach Rhoda's face and planted a kiss on her cheek.

During that week Angela behaved as if she was a slave. She cleaned, she cooked, she shopped and she even cleaned Rhoda's car. Every minute of her day was dedicated to looking after Rhoda. Angela had suggested she share Rhoda's bed so she could stay up late working in the studio, and Rhoda had agreed. Every night before Rhoda got into bed, Angela massaged her feet. Rhoda thought she was in heaven. A new life was emerging. Rhoda found herself fantasizing about having a relationship with the model. Rhoda was happy to share her life with someone, although she usually enjoyed her solitude. Perhaps she had been on her own for too long. They walked together, they ate together and they laughed together. Yes, Rhoda was happy.

The end of the week was coming closer, but Rhoda wasn't aware of it as she was busy dreaming. What if Angela had some feelings for her? What if Angela was willing to have a lesbian relationship? Why was Angela being so warm and nice towards her? Rhoda had hopes. Although, she was in her forties, she still was a good-looking woman. Rhoda had looked after herself, apart from some silly periods in her life during which she had smoked, drank and eaten meat. She now limited her alcohol intake, ate the right food, exercised and had a positive outlook on life. All these had contributed to maintaining her good looks. She was a tall woman, her body was firm and muscular. She had warm honey coloured eyes which matched her well kept short hair. Maybe Angela cared for her...

Many times during the last two weeks, Rhoda had felt like kissing Angela but she hadn't. Rhoda never made an approach to a straight woman unless she was sure that she was wanted. With Angela, things were different. Although, always nice and friendly, Angela gave mixed messages. She seemed to give her the "come on" with her eyes and when she was about to get close, she moved away. Sometimes she lightly touched Rhoda's hands and when she was about to hold hers, Angela took them away. Why? Rhoda was angry with herself. A dyke for a long time, with many deep and long , and short and light relationships, she was unable to decide whether Angela wanted her or not! After so much mental turmoil, she decided not to pressure things and let events take their natural course. In the meantime, she was determined to enjoy every minute of Angela's company. She was going to take pleasure from her mind and body.

Rhoda had finished teaching her evening class, and was looking forward to getting home. Angela was there waiting for her. She drove fast through the traffic packed Sydney streets. She stopped at a corner shop and bought some flowers for Angela. She walked intothe house. The C.D. wasn't on. Angela wasn't around. Where was she? Had Angela found another place to live? Was she bored with her? Many thoughts went through Rhoda's head. Angela was in the bedroom. She was lying on the bed crying.

"What's wrong?" she asked giving her the flowers. Ignoring the flowers, Angela hysterically demanded Rhoda's help.

"You've got to help me! I need your help! You're the only person that can do it!"

"What's happening? What's wrong?" Rhoda inquired holding Angela in her arms.

"My brother, my brother is in trouble. He was found in possession of stolen goods. I need two thousand for his bail."

"Calm down, calm down", Rhoda said as she thought."Why do you have to pay his bail? You never told me you had a brother."

"I never wanted to talk about him. He has been a bit of a rebel. I don't get on with him."

"So, why do you have to bail him?"

"Because of Mum. He is her favourite. Mum is sick and if she gets upset, she may have a heart attack."

"You didn't tell me either about your mother. Well never mind. You have the $500 I paid you for modelling, so you only need $1,500. But how come they didn't help you when you needed it?" Rhoda asked this with a hint of anger in her voice.

"Oh! Rhoda darling...",Angela said resting her head on Rhoda's chest and hugging her. "You don't understand. Lets not talk about it anymore. Come I'll run a hot bath for you".

Rhoda bewildered by what Angela had said a few minutes ago, followed her as if in a trance. Angela prepared the bath while she undressed. Neither of them said a word. The water falling on the tub made a monotonous sound which prevented Rhoda from thinking clearly. The bathroom was foggy with steam and so was her mind. Rhoda got into the tub and Angela knelt on the side. She took a face cloth. She put some soap on it and started to wash Rhoda. Rhoda closed her eyes to enjoy the pleasure of Angela's hand through the cloth. What will happen next? she wondered.

The warmth of the water and Angela's hand excited her. Angela washed her arms, her backs, her legs, and with very slow motions she went from her belly to her genitals pressing very gently against Rhoda's clitoris. Rhoda started to breath heavily. Angela smiled, threw the washer in and said:

"O.K, get ready, I've got something baking in the oven. Rhoda swallowed saliva. She was shivering. She ached, the sweet aching of passion.

They did not talk much during dinner. Rhoda was engulfed in her thoughts, trying to make sense of Angela and her behaviour. Angela appeared absent and worried. Rhoda was filling the dishwasher when Angela said:

"Do you care for me or not?"

Rhoda was tempted to say that she cared a lot. That she wanted her to stay and share, not only her house, but also her life. But she didn't.

"Why are you asking?"

"I need the money Rhoda. If you really care for me you'll give me the money without asking too many questions." Rhoda remained silent for a few minutes. Ten years ago she would have said to Angela to piss off. Today she couldn't. Had age softened her? Had the many lonely months affected her?

"OK You'll have the money tomorrow."

The next day Rhoda placed the cash in Angela's hand without asking any questions.

"I'll see you shortly", Angela said putting the money in her big bag. She kissed Rhoda on her cheek and left. Rhoda felt lonely already.

Four days had passed and Angela had not returned. The house seemed empty. Her studio was like a dried well. Her bedroom a desert of stones. Her life a misery, she had lost the will to work, to teach, to draw. All she could do was to think of Angela. On the fifth day, she showed up. She was wearing new clothes. The model looked beautiful. The mysterious eyes and the uncontrollable curly hair seemed blacker and shinier. Rhoda, unable to control herself, walked towards her and embraced her, pressing her really tight against her body as she murmured: "Darling I missed you!"

Angela pushed her away as she said:

"What ar'you doing Rhoda? Don't be silly! You know I'm not like that!" Rhoda turned around and walked towards the window. "It's a lovely night. Angela do you want to go for a walk?"

"Sorry Rhoda I came back to get my clothes", she said as she walked into the bedroom. Rhoda observed her as she collected the few things she had .

"Are you leaving me?", Rhoda asked?

"Look Rhoda, I don't know what you thought but...I'll be honest with you. The money was to bail out Frank not my brother. All these weeks away from him made me realise that I love him. I found out that he was in trouble so, I decided to help him. We'll pay you back as soon as we make some money. It will take a while because he has to keep clean. He promised me that he will look for a job. He was a bit upset that I had left him. He went mad when he found out that I was living in the house of a lesbian, but he has forgiven me. He's a great guy!"

"See ya one of these days!", she shouted as she walked through the front door with her little bundle of clothes.

Through the window Rhoda saw her get into a hotted up Holden. She took a deep breath. Angela's cheap perfume was still lingering in her nose. She sighed as two big tears rolled down her face. "I'll go for a walk in King St", she thought.

SHE CAME FROM THE SOUTH

Judith sat looking out of the attic window in the small town at the foot of the mountains. The picturesque town and the ever changing colours of the mountains gave Judith a certain solace. It was autumn, a time of the year in which everything looked as if it was painted with gold and ochre colours. Even the federation houses appeared to reflect the umber tones. The town looked at its best during this season. Oh! how much Margie had enjoyed their first autumn away from the city. Margie had spent those first few months painting non stop, as if she had a premonition, that she never was going to be able to paint again. Judith wanted Margie to discuss with her how they were going to renovate the old cottage. What colours were they going to paint each room, or how they were going to change the garden? But all Margie wanted to do was to paint in the attic. Two years ago when the Real Estate Agent showed them the cottage they decided to buy it as it had all the features they were looking for. They especially liked the big garden which Judith was going to turn back into a native garden and the attic which had a view of the mountain and enough space for both of them to work together: Margie painting and Judith writing.

Yes, it was only two years ago when they moved into the cottage. They considered themselves to be so lucky as they were able to leave their jobs and move to the country. Both have had properties in Sydney which they sold at incredible profit, making enough money to buy the cottage and to invest the rest to secure a steady income. After six months in the country Margie started to feel sick. It wasn't anything really specific. One day she would feel tired. Another she would feel dizzy. Sometimes she would not feel like eating anything. Other times she vomited everything she had eaten. Judith kept telling her to go to the doctor but she didn't want to because there were no female doctors in the little country town. Then suddenly she started to lose weight.

Judith did not notice it at first but one day she realised Margie's clothes were hanging from her. That day Margie vomited blood.

They did not speak much during the trip to Sydney. Margie's doctor had arranged for her to go straight into hospital. The next day they found out the terrifying diagnosis. Margie had cancer so advanced that it was inoperable. From then on time went by very quickly. Judith could not believe the diagnosis and tried everything she could think of to stop Margie's illness. Judith took Margie to alternative medicine centres. They became vegetarians. They learned to meditate, but it was too late. One cold night Margie died in Judith's arms. She smiled to her as if saying "don't worry".

From that day on Judith had been dead in life. In the attic she felt closer to Margie. She would hold Margie's brushes as if she was holding her hand. Hour after hour, day after day, she spent in the same place, in the same position, looking out expecting to see Margie coming up from town. Sometimes she did not even get dressed. She would get up in her nightie and dressing gown and went to bed in the same clothes. Many of their friends had come to support her but she had asked them to leave. She wanted to be on her own with her memories . After a while her friends gave up and no one turned up at the country cottage anymore. She drank coffee and went back to smoking. She only went down to town when she run out of cigarettes or other essential items such as coffee and sugar. Judith was not interested in anything anymore, not even her writing which had once been very important to her. She had not cleaned the house in months and the weeds had taken over the once manicured lawns and gardens. She had forgotten many times to feed her cat Dulcie, so Dulcie was now spending most of her time at the neighbour's house who owned two cats and always left out plenty of food. Judith did not care, Judith had lost her will to live. She had no dreams, no illusions. She was as dead as Margie.

One day that autumn, Judith was cursing herself because she had no courage to end her life, when she saw her coming up the road from the south. She was tall and young. She was carrying a backpack. She seemed tired. She was walking slowly and with her back arched. Judith thought that the backpack was too heavy and big for such a thin person. She wondered where the young woman was going as only her cottage and the one with the cats were at the end of the winding road. Around the last bend the young woman walked faster as if wanting to arrive quicker to her destination. From there on the young woman disappeared from sight. A few minutes later her doorbell was ringing. Judith gave a jump when she heard it. How was it possible? She was not waiting for anyone. On the way down to open the door she saw herself in the mirror hanging in the hallway. She could not believe that the reflection she was looking at was her own. She had dark rings around her eyes. Her hair had no style or proper length. It was neither long nor short, but that awful length somewhere between the end of the ears and the shoulders. She had not been to the hairdresser in months. Her hair looked dry, even dirty. The expression on her face was pitiful. She had aged so much! The bell rang again. She hurried downstairs and opened the door. There, on her front porch was standing the young woman with the backpack.

Judith and the woman looked at each other. After a few seconds Judith broke the silence.

"You are in the wrong place", she said with difficulty as she had not spoken to anyone in days.

"No, I think I'm in the right place. You need a gardener and someone to do odd jobs", said the young woman with a very unusual accent and as she rested her backpack.

"Who told you?" Judith blurted with anger.

"No offence! I need work and a place to stay. I can see that you need a gardener and some painting needs to be done.. I am a very good gardener. I can do all sorts of repairs. Don't worry about money. Just a bed and food is enough. I am very tired, please. I won't bother you.

Uou won't even know I'm around. I will work very quietly" pleaded the woman with the accent. For some reason Judith felt sorry for the young traveller and agreed to let her stay. She showed her in and led her to one of the spare bedrooms downstairs. She told her that she had to cook for herself as she was sick and was not going to do it. Ximena thanked Judith and promised that she was going to be happy with her work.

That night Judith slept peacefully, usually the emotional pain and the loneliness stopped her from relaxing. The fact that there was someone in the house made her feel at ease. The next day she woke up when she felt a gentle tap on her shoulder. She opened her eyes and she saw Ximena standing next to her with a tray.

"Buenos Dias! Good morning! Your breakfast is ready". Judith, like an automaton, sat on the bed and took the tray. Ximena opened the curtains and the window and left the room. On the tray, a beautiful breakfast had been presented: eggs, fresh baked scones and orange juice. She wondered where Ximena had got the ingredients from as she had no food left in the house. She felt obliged to eat the food, although she was not hungry.

Judith felt good after eating the breakfast. She decided to get dressed and go down to town to buy some food. That poor kid needed to eat! After having a shower, she looked for something to wear. She realised then that she had not done any washing for months. She felt embarrassed. She went around her bedroom, and the other rooms collecting all her dirty clothes. She was going to take them to the laundromat. Although she drove there and back, the trip to town left her exhausted. When she arrived, Ximena rushed to the car to help her with the parcels. As they walked in, Judith noticed that Ximena had cleaned the whole house. There were flowers in all the vases and a nice smell was coming from the oven.

They sat down for lunch. Judith then found out that while she was sleeping Ximena had gone to town and bought all the necessary food for breakfast. Judith wanted to refund her the money but Ximena refused to take it. Judith asked her a few questions which Ximena answered with long and elaborate answers. Ximena was travelling around Australia before deciding in which city to settle. She was from Chile. Her father was German and her mother Spanish / Indian. She was a Landscape Architect and was hoping in the future to be able to work in her field. She had grown up in a farm where she learned all the handy work she knew. After lunch Judith went back to the attic. From her window, she could see the dark and beautiful woman working in the garden. By the end of the afternoon, the front garden was looking a lot better. Ximena was fast and efficient. She left no place in the house unclean, but it was not just surface cleaning. She even took curtains down to be dry cleaned and rugs, mattresses, blankets were hung in the sun "in order to get rid of germs" Ximena had some interesting ideas!

When Ximena found out that Judith was a writer she pleaded with her to read her aloud all her works. Judith could not deny this to Ximena as she was such a nice person. Every night after dinner they sat in front of the fire with cookies and chocolate for reading sessions. Ximena loved Judith's writings, and as she read, she made appropriate comments. She laughed or sighed at the right time. Ximena was a Lesbian too and Judith was thrilled when she found out. One night she just said it and went on to tell Judith how she had become a dyke and how sad she was when her first girlfriend left her for a man. Now after many relationships, she had grown hard in her heart. That same night Ximena said that she had a confession to make. Judith was eager to know. Ximena asked her wait a moment and went into her room coming back with an envelope in her hand. She handed the envelope to Judith and to her surprise it was addressed to her. She opened the envelope and read the letter it contained. It was a letter from one of her friends to introduce Ximena to her, saying how good and efficient she was, and how it could be beneficial for both them if she gave lodging to the young Chilean. Judith was shocked and wanted to know why she had not shown her the letter before. Ximena said that if she had shown her the letter, she probably would have felt obliged to help her but now she knew for sure that Judith really wanted to help the young traveller. They both laughed and continued with their talks. That night Judith could not go to sleep. She was feeling guilty. How could she have laughed when Margie was dead? She cried again as she had not done since Ximena had arrived.

After refusing the breakfast that Ximena had brought her, Judith went back to the attic. She sat there as she used to , holding Margie's brushes and going over and over in her mind the memories that she had of Margie. It was around ten p.m. when Ximena came into the attic. She knelt next to Judith and holding her hands said:

"By thinking of her you won't bring her back. I know how much you are suffering. Don't you think that she would like you to go on with your life?"

"What do you know? How do you know about Margie?", asked Judith with anger in her voice.

"It's no use to get angry with me or anyone. Your friend Pat from Sydney told me about your lover's death. She told me with no malice. She warned me to be prepared." Judith's initial anger dissipated. Ximena was so strong and gentle, so supporting. Her words were soothing and comforting. Ximena talked and talked with her heavy accent but with words that really touched Judith's inner core. Ximena took Judith to bed, helped her to undress and to lie down. She sat on the bed next to her and caressed Judith's forehead until she went to sleep.

The next morning, Ximena cheerfully woke her up and stood there until she ate the breakfast demanding that she get dressed immediately as they had to go to town. Judith wanted to protest but Ximena was not listening. Judith wanted to know were they were going. It was a surprise. Ximena asked Judith if she could drive the van and Judith allowed her. Judith did not say a word during the trip into town. They stopped in a parking lot and walked towards the main street. "Here we are", said Ximena holding Judith's arm and pushing her into a beauty salon. Judith had no time to protest since the hairdresser was waiting for them. She grabbed Judith and got her to sit down. Ximena asked the hairdresser when to come back. " In two hours your friend will be ready", the woman said. Judith did not have to say a word as Ximena already had arranged the hair cut she should have and for a facial and massage. The hairdresser explained to Judith that her friend had come yesterday and paid and told them what to do with her. The hairdresser made silly comments like "Oh you have a real good friend eh?" Judith was surprised with herself and with Ximena. With herself because she seemed to have lost all the power of making decisions, and with Ximena because of the control that she was exerting over her.

Two hours later Ximena was standing by the door. Judith was saying thank you to the beauty therapist who had given her the facial and the massage. Once in the car Ximena did not stop telling her how beautiful she looked with her new hair style. Judith was embarrassed by Ximena's exclamations. That night they drank champagne and ate the vegetarian banquet that Ximena had prepared with the help of Judith. They had fun cooking and exchanging recipes. Judith wanted to learn about South American food and Ximena wanted to learn about Australian food. Like some other nights they sat in front of the fire, Judith reading to Ximena all her "deep" and erotic sexual poems.

A few days later, Ximena had another surprise for Judith. Again she had to eat and dress quickly. The orders were to wear jeans and runners. Ximena had found two old bicycles in the toolshed and she had repaired them. From then on every morning, after breakfast, they went cycling to the neighbouring towns. During these trips they looked at gardens, churches, cemeteries and old houses. Sometimes, when the weather was good they went bush walking, or riding horses or for picnics up the highest mountain.

By now it was spring. Judith had given up smoking under the watchful eye of Ximena. Her skin glowed. She had put on some weight and she looked strong and healthy. Judith was not only eating the right food but also doing her daily quota of exercises, whether aerobics under the instruction of Ximena, jogging or cycling. Pushed by Ximena, she was now writing an hour a day. Judith rarely went to the attic anymore. She wrote in the kitchen or in the dining room while Ximena read, cooked or cleaned.

It was Judith's birthday, so Ximena planned a celebration. She decorated the dining room with spring flowers and paper ribbons. She baked a cake and cooked a dinner that Judith said was fit for a queen. They dined by candlelight and drank champagne until they became giggly and silly. Ximena suggested that they dance. Judith agreed and put on one of her old records. They danced cheek to cheek. Judith was shorter than Ximena, but only by a few centimetres. Her forehead reached Ximena's chin. Ximena was leading. They laughed and joked . Ximena made fun of Judith because the record was so old! Suddenly, Ximena stopped laughing, bent her head and kissed Judith on the mouth. Judith, in that moment realised how much she had wanted to kiss the young woman but she never had the courage to do so. Judith opened her mouth allowing Ximena's tongue to desperately search for hers. Their tongues joined in a passionate kiss, while their bodies palpitated in each other's arms. Judith's hand caressed Ximena's breast. With gentle strokes, she touched the young and erect nipples. Ximena's hands were now getting to know Judith's body with the passion that she had contained for months. When their passion reached a point in which neither of them could stand any longer, they lay on the carpet and made love to each other. While making love, the memory of Margie crossed Judith's mind, but this time no guilt feelings invaded her. Ximena had convinced her that she was alive and as such she had to live intensely and furiously. Ximena had instilled in her, the idea, that it is the duty of all of those who are blessed with life and health to live each minute of their life as if it was their last. Judith and Ximena made love many times after that day.

Then Summer came...

Ximena had been quiet and subdued for some days. When Judith had asked her what was wrong she had said that she was okay. But Judith knew that something was wrong. That night Judith, convincing her that they were friends above everything else, and that she should trust her, encouraged her to talk. Ximena with sadness in her voice told Judith that it was time for her to move on. In her heart Judith knew that one day she was going to go.

Two weeks later from the attic, Judith saw Ximena walk down to town, her back arched with the weight of the backpack. Judith was sad but she was dry of tears. All her tears had been spilled for Margie. But, hidden amongst her sadness a tiny spark was growing. A spark which was growing out of the seed that Ximena had planted. Judith had learned to live again, to love and to be happy. When Ximena's figure had disappeared from her view, she went to the telephone. She had many calls to make. She was going to sell the cottage. She was going back to Sydney: to her friends, to her teaching career, to her professional writing, to all that once had made her happy. Judith was going back to life because of the woman who had came from the south. Ximena had taught her to live again.

THE CULT

I never imagined that my life was going to change in such a radical way when Paul, the editor of the newspaper where I work as a journalist, gave me my next assignment. "Here", he said, as he handed me a piece of paper with a name and a telephone number scribbled on it. "Check them out. We may get a good story out of them." "Who are they?" I asked ingenuously. "They 're a bunch of lunatics as far as I can gather. They're a women's sect. As you know, anything to do with cults, witches, or the occult always make a good story. New age stuff sells papers."

No! Definitely, I did not need a new assignment when my life was in such a turmoil. I cannot work when I have a broken heart. Santiago, the guy whom I have shared my bed and my life with for the last nine months, was packing his bags to go back to Chile. He had tried to settle here, but he couldn't.

"You Australians are too cold!" he used to say. I never knew what he meant because I gave him more than I had ever given to any other guy. I gave him all my love and dedication. I even went to the point of learning how to say "Adios amigo", and to cook "Chilli Con Carne".

I was devastated. Santiago was one of the many guys with whom I had started a relationship that went nowhere. My ego was deflated since I thought it was my fault that I couldn't keep a man. They all accused me of being too independent, or too bossy, or too cold in bed. Now I realised that there was not a thing wrong with me. The assignment came at the wrong time, since I was about to ask for two weeks holiday. I wanted to go away to Bali, or to Fiji, to forget Santiago, the bastard, but I was too slow and never got around to asking for the time off.

With the bit of paper still in my hand, I sat at my desk feeling sorry for myself. I looked up and I saw a message on my terminal. "How about a weekend up in Foster? It's my parents wedding anniversary, and they are throwing a big party. If yes, ring me tonight. I'll be leaving at 7 a.m. I hope you'll come." Why not! I said to myself, I needed to get away and I had no weekend assignment. I read the name on the piece of paper, LEANNE GARLAND *f* MANAGER. For some reason I felt a compulsion to telephone her and make the appointment for Saturday, but I decided to leave it for the next week. So I went to Foster. When I arrived back on Sunday night, Santiago had left. I went to bed and cried until I fell asleep.

That night, I had the weirdest dream I saw Santiago on a donkey, crossing the Andes, and I was behind him carrying his bags. I dreamt also of an unknown beautiful woman. She was all dressed in black. She was wearing a seethrough tunic. Her hair was red like fire. I looked at her and noticed that her eyes were also red. When I realised that her eyes were red, I panicked and shivering I woke up.

I went back to sleep, and to my surprise, the dream continued. The woman with the red hair and eyes told me, in an authoritarian voice, "You don't need him! You're a strong female. Don't feel sorry for yourself." This time I did not panic because her words, although authoritarian in tone, were very soothing. I slept peacefully until the next day.

When I woke up I was expecting to be upset, or sad, or angry, or something negative and awful, but that was not the case. I was feeling great! I felt very cheerful and looking forward to going to work. It was going to be good to have the apartment all to myself. I was determined to be happy with or without Santiago. Life is always full of joys and surprises. I arrived at the office around 9.30. Everyone looked grey and doomed, as they always do on Monday mornings. I sat at my desk and looked for the number in order to ring Leanne.

When Leanne returned my call, her voice sounded familiar. She did not want to talk over the telephone. "Come to my place at 8 p.m. ", she said, and gave me an address in Paddington. I thought that maybe I knew her, although I was quite sure that I have never met anyone called Leanne Garland. I have an excellent memory for names and faces, a fact that has helped me in my profession.

For some reason, that morning, I was very distracted. I couldn't concentrate. All my thoughts were focused on the appointment I had with Leanne. I tried to work on another feature article, which I had been assigned a while ago, but which I kept putting off because I found it so bloody boring "The Validity of IQ Tests" Yuk!

After many attempts at getting involved in IQ tests, I picked up my handbag, my tape recorder and left the office. I wasn't any longer depressed. I should have been. The man I thought was going to be the man of my life, had left me. I must be getting used to being fucked and dumped, I said to myself. I was nevertheless feeling empty. For a long time until now, I had refused to fill this sort of inner hole with food. Now I fill it with clothes, books and scarves. I took the bus and went to the greatest store in town, David Jones. I spent two glorious hours and about three hundred dollars.

When I got home, the wound opened up again. The apartment looked bare and lonely. I was about to start crying when I remembered my 8 p.m. appointment. It was then 6 o'clock. I had a bite to eat and a long, long shower. I wanted to look good. Leanne sounded efficient, managerial and educated. I imagined her in power dressing gear. I didn't want to feel underdressed in her presence. By 7.30 I was ready and happy with the way I looked.

Feeling secure with my new clothes, I picked up my working tools and drove to Paddo. I was early, so I sat in the car observing the house. It was one of the best in the street: a two storey fully renovated terrace. I was anxious. I felt like a cigarette, although I haven't had one for nearly two years.

When Leanne opened the door I nearly fainted. Leanne looked exactly like the woman in my dream. Well, almost exactly, because she didn't have red eyes. They were brown. She must have noticed my look of surprise because she smiled and took me by the hand and lead me into the house. It took me a few minutes to compose myself. Leanne's presence was overwhelming. It was as if some sort of power emanated from her. Finally I dragged the words out of my mouth.

"Well...as you know... I'm here... to discuss an article on your group...cult...? "I said.

"I didn't want to tell you over the telephone, but we do not grant interviews, or allow people to write about us, unless they comply with our conditions", Leanne said in a very friendly tone.

"Conditions?", I asked.

"Yes, for you to be able to write the article you must become part of our group", she answered.

I couldn't believe what I was hearing. I smiled as I told her that I was not interested in becoming a member of her little coven, I was there following orders. Leanne seemed to expect my reply which she ignored because she kept talking as if I had accepted.

"In order to become a member of our group you have to pass three trials and I must warn you, only very few women pass them. You need to be a particular kind of woman. I suspected you would say no on the first instance, but I'm sure you'll change your mind!", she said.

Was this a challenge? I found out later that Leanne has a sixth sense that allows her to sum up people in a few minutes. Yes, it was a challenge and she knew I was going to take it. Although at the time, I said I was not interested. She showed me to the door and we shook hands. "I'll see you soon!". Witch! I thought. You'll never see me again. I was back the next day!

That night I couldn't sleep thinking of the challenge Leanne had suggested. My life needed excitement. Maybe it was a good idea to take the assignment. After tossing and tossing in bed for hours, pondering about the damned coven, I decided to take up the challenge.

The next day, when I telephoned Leanne to make another appointment, she said that she was waiting for my call. We arranged to meet that same night. This time, I wasn't anxious, I was intrigued. So there I was, sitting in Leanne's posh and tastefully decorated lounge room, hanging on to each and every one of her words.

With her deep voice and staring into my eyes she said:

"This isn't an ordinary group. We are very special women, and we only talk about our principles, rules, and blessings ..."

"Blessings?", I interrupted.

"Yes, yes blessings. We only talk about our secrets to women who are part of our group. Only women can be part of our group."

"What I don't understand, is how can anyone be part of your group if you don't tell anyone about it?", I asked.

Arching her eyebrows Leanne answered"You'll be surprised. We don't need to go out to recruit members.They come to us, just like you! We do not need money or women who don't meet our standards".

"Follow me!", she ordered, without giving me time to ask any other question. Again, she held my hand, but this time something like an electrical current, travelled through my spine when I felt her skin over mine. It gave me eerie but pleasurable feelings. I stood up and followed her. She took me right through the house and into a big room.

With curiosity I looked around. Two big windows were dressed with heavy black curtains. Everything in that room was either black or red. Candles, dozens of them, flickered in unison. There were big cushions all over the floor. In a corner, there was some sort of altar. I couldn't see who the deity represented in the statue. I know now who she is, but I'm not allowed to write her name, as it goes against Her ancient codes and mandates. A heavy scented incense was burning in a brass vase.

We sat on two cushions. Leanne sat with her legs crossed in the lotus position. I sat with great difficulty I was wearing high heals and a very uncomfortable, too tight mini skirt. She was wearing a tunic, similar to the red one she had had on in my dream. Through the thin and light material I could see her breast. I felt like touching them!

To be a member of this exclusive group, I had to pass three trials Leanne had said. Once I passed the trials, she was going to reveal to me all the secrets of the group so I could write the article. Looking directly into my eyes, she asked me if I was ready for my first trial. I said that I was. When she told me what the first trial was, I nearly chocked on my own saliva.

"You are to contact this psychologist, who will administer to you an IQ test. Once you have the results of the test, bring them to me. Then I'll tell you whether you'll be allowed to take the second and third trial ", Leanne said, handing me a card with the name of the Psychologist.

I wanted to protest. I wanted to tell her that IQ tests were a lot of rubbish, but before I could open my mouth she was standing next to me. Leanne had placed her hands above my head, and with her eyes closed, she recited some sort of prayer in a language that I could not identify. Her hands were on my head, and although she was not touching me, they were exerting an incredible force. Slowly, a feeling of warmth that was coming from her hands inundated my whole being. What happened next I don't know. All I remember is that I was sleeping very peacefully on the cushions. When Leanne woke me up, she told me to go home because it was late. "You needed that rest", she said. I looked at my watcht. It was1 a.m.in the morning I had slept for four hours.

Next morning, I woke up believing that all this mumbo jumbo was ridiculous. I was going to tell Paul that the article was never going to see the light, because the cult members were a bunch of silly women, not worth writing about. By breakfast time I had changed my mind, and hurried to make the appointment with the famous Psychologist Beatriz Copello. Was I going mad? Had Leanne drugged me? Why was I so keen to continue with this silly affair? Why couldn't I get Leanne out of my mind? Why did I want to caress Leanne's breast? I had to wait fifteen days to get an appointment with the psychologist. She was fully booked and I was lucky that she had a cancellation.

Beatriz was very friendly and professional. She explained to me the nature of the test and its validity. After talking to her, I was convinced that these tests were valuable if given to the people that they were designed for white Anglo*f*Saxons. I was very excited now about doing the IQ test. Having a different opinion about IQ tests, I went back to my other forgotten article.

Beatriz told me that an IQ of 140 was excellent considering that the average person has a IQof 100. She gave me a written report that now I treasure. After having so many relationships that had failed, I used to think that I was silly. Holding the report next to my heart, I telephoned Leanne.

"You made it", she said in a happy voice, and added "It would have been a pity if you didn't make it because I like you very much. We only accept women with a minimum IQ of 120."

I was angry, furious, ready to slap Leanne's pretty face. Who did those women think they were? Bloody elitists!

I was very angry but I did not say anything, and went that night, to give her a copy of the psychological report. This time we sat in her vogue style lounge room. She seemed in a hurry. She did not ask me to sit down. I was disappointed because I wanted to talk to her, to get to know her and to get close to Leanne.

She had a diary in her hands. She flicked through the pages and asked me if next Friday at 10 p.m. was alright for my next trial. I said it was fine. Before I left she handed me an envelope. Once in the car I opened it. It had a cheque with a little note saying that it was the refund for the money I had spent at the Psychologist's.

As usual, when you wait for a day to come the time seems never to pass. That week I kept myself busy catching up with friends and going to the movies. I didn't want to be by myself because Leanne had become an obsession. Finally, Friday arrived. At one minute to ten, I knocked at Leanne's door. I was surprised when someone else opened the door.

"Hi! I'm Amadea. I was waiting for you. Please follow me! " said the young woman who looked like a Greek Goddess. I followed her. Amadea guided me through the same corridor that led to the altar room. Amadea opened a side door, and asked me to enter. She closed the door behind me with a key. The room was very small. It had no furniture or windows ƒonly a small bronze tray was placed on a corner. On the tray rested a little cup and a candle burned on a bronze candle holder.

I don't know how long I stood there. After two or three hours, I started to panic. Noone knew that I was there. Anyone could have killed me very easily. I imagined that these women were crazy fanatics, who killed stupid people like me, whose curiosity was greater than their sense of protection.

I was about to start screaming when a small white envelope was passed to me from under the door. I ripped the envelope and took the small note in which Leanne or someone had written:

"DRINK YOUR SISTER'S BLOOD FROM THE BRONZE GOBLET. THIS WILL GIVE YOU POWER AND WILL ALLOW YOU TO BE PART OF US IN THE NAME OF OUR BLESSED GODDESS."

My legs were hurting, my heart was pounding and my mouth had dried. I walked to the bronze cup and I sat on the floor looking at its content. I smelt the content and assumed it was blood, perhaps menstrual blood! I questioned my sanity and theirs. I put the cup on the floor and as I did this the room started to fill with a dense smoke.

I wanted to get out, to run away, to leave behind this unusual assignment. Surprisingly, instead of kicking the door until someone opened it, I took the cup and in a mouthful I drank the contents. It tasted salty but also sweet as well. The smoke had stopped coming in. I was ready to relax when suddenly I heard tiny footsteps.

From a very small opening at the bottom of the back wall, rats, about fifteen centimetres long, raced into the room. I counted ten of the hideous rodents which started to run around the room as though chased by a cat. So this was the second trial!

I must admit that I don't like rats, but I was not going to go crazy or yell just because ten rats surrounded me. As for menstrual blood, well... it's not as bad as men want the world to believe it is. I was thinking about this when my head commenced to spin around. The blood must have been mixed with some sort of drug because I passed out. When I woke up I was in my own bed. Yes! In my own bed in my flat.

After the initial shock of waking up in my own bed, I realised that I was so sexually excited that my insides were burning. My clitoris was in pain and my vagina was palpitating with desire. I was still feeling a bit giddy I assumed it was still the effect of the drug.

In my mind's eye I saw Leanne. Her image increased my excitement. I turned around, and around a thousand times trying to forget her. A new feeling was taking over me *f* the desire to touch Leanne, to be near her, to feel her body with my body.

As if guided by a mysterious force, my hand reached for my clitoris, and I stroked it gently and slowly. I was very wet. I imagined Leanne's body. I imagined kissing her beautiful breast. I imagined penetrating her with my fingers, feeling the velvet of her insides. In my mind I kissed her lips, her neck, her whole body. With my tongue I titillated her clitoris.

I never had been so excited. Neither had I been excited by the thought of making love to a woman. Then I came. I had the most intense and satisfying orgasm ever. Before going to sleep, I pondered about my sexuality.

With anxiety, I admitted that I had always had feelings for women, and that I had pushed them to the back of my mind, ignoring them. I realised then that my sexuality must have been the reason for the failure of my relationships with men. Never, up to that date, had I had a fulfilling and happy sex life. I went to sleep with the sweet thought that maybe I was a lesbian.

The next morning, as I opened my eyes, an incredible guilt feeling descended over me. I had definitely gone mad. Sometimes people go mad for no reason. Was I really a lesbian? Was I being indoctrinated into a weird sect? Was it all a dream? I needed to test the reality of my existence. I decided to call my mother. She answered in a sleepy voice.

"It's me Mum!"

"What's wrong darling? she asked.

"I just wanted to know how are you?"

"Well sweety, did you have a bad dream?"

"I'm not sure Mum?"

"Why don't you ring me again later and we'll chat about it?

"Later?"

"Well Deborah it's 4.30 AM !" It was indeed.

After apologising and promising my mother to ring later I had a shower. I got dressed and went out for a walk. I had to get clear in my mind the events of the last few weeks. Walking helps me to think clearly.

A week had passed since the night of the rats. During that week, I changed my opinion many times about Leanne, the group, and myself.

My life was in a turmoil again. The articles were not finished and Paul was driving me mad. My friends were worried about me. Everyone kept asking me what was wrong. Mum kept ringing everyday and asking me to visit her. Meantime all I wanted was to see Leanne, be with her, admire her, love her... Yes, I discovered that I was in love with her.

Another week passed. After a trying day at the office, in which Paul told me to deliver the goods or I was getting out of the paper, the telephone rang. It was Amadea. She told me that they would be waiting for me the day after tomorrow, which was Friday at 10P.M. I spent all Thursday and Friday finishing the IQ article. Paul was happy with it, and said that he was joking when he said that he was going to get rid of me. "You're the best babe!" he said. Sexist creep!

That afternoon, I went for drinks with some of my work mates. After an hour at the pub I went home and prepared myself physically and mentally for my last trial. I was dying to see Leanne! Again I arrived at Leanne's at one minute to ten. Leanne opened the door. She was wearing a red see through tunic like the one she was wearing in my dream.

I still could not get over how I dreamt about her before I had even meet her. Leanne later explained to me that it is in the astral world where all the relationships are forged. But back to that night. When I saw Leanne my heart gave a jump and my eyes travelled through her body. She had no underwear! Leanne smiled and I shivered.

"Come!", she said in her commanding but appealing voice. "Tonight is your last trial. I hope you will enjoy it", she added.

"Enjoy?" I asked. No answer. She smiled again. We walked through the long corridor that led to the altar room. Mozart's music could be heard. As soon as my eyes adapted to the darkness, I noticed that other women were there. The light of the candles and the incense gave the room a mysterious atmosphere.

In the middle of the room, all the cushions had been brought together. Six women were ther. They were all dressed in the same way as Leanne.

Three women were kneeling on the left side of the cushions, and three on the opposite side. They all smiled at me when I entered the room.

No one said anything. One of them went to the altar and picked up a tiny cup which she offered to me. I drank the contents without hesitation. Leanne, with the help of the woman who had brought me the glass undressed me. I couldn't excuse myself, leave the room, ring my mother to check whether I was dreaming or not. Without me uttering a single complain, guided me to the cushions and asked me to lie down. Whatever they had given me to drink made me feel as if I was on top of the world. I was relaxed but excited at the same time. I was very curious about my third trial.

As I lay down, the five women caressed me. Each of them seemed to be in charge of giving pleasure to a particular part of the body. The one in charge of my feet massage them, tickled them gently, and finally kissed them. Two of them were looking after my arms, and gave them the same treatment *f* caresses, kisses, licks and so on. Leanne stroke my forehead very gently.

I couldn't believe that feeling such pleasure was possible. Leanne's hands went down very slowly from my shoulder to my breast, then to my belly, and stopping at the beginning of my pubic hair. I was aroused as I never had been before. I started to moan and breathe heavily.

Suddenly my Catholic upbringing turned up unexpectedly and guilt feelings invaded me. Was this an orgy? Was all this morally correct? As if she was reading my mind, Leanne said "Don't worry about anything. Just enjoy the experience. You are now another sister under the protection of our Goddess".

What Leanne said sounded right. I, just lay there enjoying the experience that my new Goddess had approved. Great! My moaning turned to screams of pleasure. When the women realised my state, they stopped caressing me and left and Leanne made love to me.

Although I was a bit self conscious because this was my first lesbian experience I did to Leanne what I had fantasised doing. I touched her, kissed her, stroked her hair, and finally became one with her. I spent the whole weekend making love with Leanne my priestess.

Yes, my life changed in a very radical way. I have a new job in a feminist newspaper. Paul sacked me when I refused to write the article about the women's' sect as he called it. Living as a lesbian and having been accepted as a full member of the group has changed me. I have learned to give love as well as to receive and I am very happy now.

Is anyone out there interested in writing an article about a women's coven?

CHACO

In those days married women did not leave their husbands. In those days married women did not even dare separate. Women who did, became outcasts. Those poor souls who, after years of suffering had the courage to leave, were considered fallen women. They were shut out of society, and everyone put them down, or ignored them. A woman's place was next to her husband and her children. In those days it was not important how bad the husband treated his wife and children. A woman's duty was to respect and obey her spouse no matter what. Those were hard times for women.

Maria Francisca Dominga had a mean husband. He was not a caring person, not even a decent one. Daily he abused her and her children. Very often the police had to bring him home in a drunken stupor. Every time he drank, he became abusive and obnoxious. He was a rich and well known man in the small town where Maria Francisca Dominga lived with her family. Nearly everyone in Vera(1) believed she was very fortunate to marry the richest man in town. Only a few knew his true self. He was a man without feelings or principles.

After years of pain and suffering, after years of thinking about leaving him and planning how to do it, she finally built the courage up to leave him and her children. She couldn't take her children with her. How was she going to support them? She knew he was not going to look after them. She was sure that as as soon as he realised that she was gone for ever, he would hand the children over to her parents. In her parents' care her children were no longer going to suffer as much.

She ran away, with $100 pesos and a pain in her heart for having abandoned her children. She caught a train and went as far as she could go with half of the money she had. Maria Francisca Dominga was now in Chaco(2), in a little hotel in El Pintado, a small town at the edge of the jungle. Behind she left her most precious treasure: her children. She had to save her children from the abuse that he so easily dispensed on them. In afew, days they were going to be living under the care and protection of her parents.

Maria Francisca Dominga had arrived at the Hotel in mid afternoon. Everyone was complaining about the heat: the porter at the train station who called the taxi for her, the taxi driver and even the hotel's concierge. She had asked for lemonade and was sipping it slowly, sitting on the large double bed. She had undressed and already had hung the few clothes she had brought with her. Her thoughts were dense and deep like the near jungle. Maria Francisca Dominga was trying not to think because she had just realised the magnitude of her act. An act

of defiance, not only against her husband, but against her family and against society. The jungle noises intermingled with her thoughts and her thoughts became jungle and the jungle became Maria Francisca Dominga.

When Maria woke up it was dark. She woke up hearing her younger boy calling her. She opened her eyes shivering with fright. Where was she? Fabian was crying. Wwhere was his cot? She did not recognise the surroundings. It took her a few minutes to come back to reality. It was nearly 8 p.m., the time when dinner was served at the hotel La Pantera. Quickly she got up and had a shower. It was still very hot, hot and humid. It was going to take hours to dry her long and thick hair, so she decided to leave it wet and tied it back with a white ribbon.

A white sun dress was appropriate for the heat. No bra, no petticoat, no husband to tell her what she should wear. She looked at herself in the mirror of the old wardrobe: she looked like a child: thirteen, fourteen perhaps. She had had three children: the first one when she was seventeen, the second one when she was eighteen and the last one at nineteen. She was now twenty, and her husband wanted more children. When he found out that she was taking contraceptives pills, he had slapped her and called her a murderer. He threw away the pills, but she got another packet from the chemist's assistant who was her best friend. She had been the one who had told her about these marvellous pills.

Only two other tables were occupied at La Pantera's Restaurant. On one, a middle aged couple and on the other a young woman. The food was tasteless but she did not care. She was thankful that she had something to eat. Probably soon she would not have any money left. $50 pesos did not last long. She knew she had to find work. As she ate, she made plans about work and a place to live.

Between mouthfuls she looked around. Through the big open doors she could see the beginning of the jungle. Maria had always fantasized about living in a hot place near the jungle. She could not understand how she could be eating while feeling so sad about having left her children. Analysing her feelings, she realised that she was not only sad but also excited, excited about the new life that was awaiting her. Maria Francisca Dominga was now free and that gave her strength to go ahead.

Maria felt that someone was looking at her. She turned around and noticed that the dark young woman had her eyes fixed on her . She smiled at her but Maria did not smile back. After dinner, she walked to the back of the hotel where she had seen some deck chairs. She sat to observe the thick vegetation and the fading colours, as the night was falling on. The mosquitoes were big and insistent, not like the ones in Vera. Her legs were by now all splattered with blood where she had squashed the annoying insects.

"It take time to be mosquito's friend. Me old grandpa say: "Don't kill them mosquitoes. Ask them nicely no to bite you, and them leave you alone. Indian tale." Maria Francisca Dominga turned her head and saw the young woman she had seen in the dining room. She felt angry about her presence. Who was she to approach her? Maria did not like to be approached by strangers. Her mother always had insisted that she did not speak to people she did not know, especially if they were not from her social class. She could tell from the colour of her skin, from the way she was dressed, and because of her unrefined accent that she was not one of her own. But were these her own beliefs or those of her old fashioned parents? Now she was on her own and could do what she wished.

The woman kept talking as she sat in the chair next to Maria.

" Them, call me Tapa (4) cause I'm short. Indian race not very tall people. Your name?". There was some sort of authority emanating from this woman, an authority that prevented Maria from behaving according to her social and racial prejudices: prejudices that she promised herself to analyse later. She was ready to start a new life and if necessary to become a different person, a person with her own ideas and attitudes.

"My name is Maria Francisca Dominga", she said after a prolonged silence.

"Long name!"

"Well my mother is a devout catholic so she named me after the Virgin Mary and St Francis".

"What about Dominga(5)?"

"I was born on a Sunday."

Both women laughed. Tapa kept talking and talking. She told Maria about the other guests in the hotel, about the owners, about the food and about the little town a few miles away from the hotel. Maria told the woman very little except that she was looking for a job. Mesmerized by the dark woman, she sat there enjoying the unusual experience.

As Tapa talked Maria observed her. She was quite short but she looked so strong! Her arms and legs were very muscular. Her hair was black and very short. Her features were different from the European' faces.

"Do you have Spanish blood in you?", Maria asked.

"You ever see a Spaniard with a nose like Tapa's? ", she said laughing . "Tapa is a Toba(6)", she added.

"You are the first indian I have ever met." Maria said .

"Tapa not surprised. The Spaniards killed most of my people. Maria Spanish?", Tapa asked with a hint of concern, thinking that perhaps she had offended Maria.

"My mother is Spanish. My father is English".

Maria could not believe that she was talking with a real Indian. She had studied about them at school but she had forgotten most of what she had learnt, although she remembered some of their beautiful legends and stories. As she was talking to Tapa, she realised that she knew so little about everything. The nuns had not given her the best of education and her parents had overprotected her so much. How mistaken she had been to think that marriage was a way out from the rigid control of her parents. Her husband had been worse than her father. But now she was free. Free! Free! Free! Finally Maria went to sleep. The heat, the mosquitoes the unusual jungle noises and the pain of not seeing her children had prevented her from sleeping. While waiting to fall sleep, she had gone over and over the conversation with Tapa. She wondered why her parents had always been so strict, forbidding her to speak or mix with girls that looked like Tapa. Some of her parent's maids had children, but she had not been allowed to play with them. Away from the power that her parents and husband had exerted on her, she enjoyed the thought of being able to mix with whom she pleased. Maria fall sleep imagining that she was reading a story to her children.

Maria Francisca Dominga had a beautiful dream: she had saved enough money and she had been given custody of the children. The laws had changed and women were allowed to keep their children, even if they had deserted the conjugal home. Flowers in the garden, the children playing with iguanas' babies and a little house at the edge of the jungle...

A gentle tap at the door woke Maria up. She looked at her wrist watch. It was 6.30 a.m.

"Tapa knocking at door. She take Maria swimming?"

Was this woman crazy? What manners did Tapa have that she dared to wake her up at this time? Swimming at 6.30 a.m.? She normally would get up at ten or eleven and have breakfast in bed. She could sleep all she wanted because the children were looked after by their nanny.

"You coming or not?" said Tapa in a commanding voice. Maria got up and opened the door. She was going to tell Tapa off for annoying her but seeing her friendly smile she, couldn't. Rubbing her eyes, she motioned for Tapa to come in.

"Tapa take you to a beautiful place. Bring towel."

"I have no swimming costume, and its too early to get up."

"If Maria want job, Maria learn to get up early. Swim good! You think Tapa take Maria to public bath? Tapa and Maria go to river Bermejo."

Maria put on her white dress, took a towel, locked her room and followed Tapa.

They walked for about twenty minutes. Tapa was wearing a white shirt with most of its buttons opened at the front. Everytime she moved the swellings of her firm breast could be seen. She was wearing green army fatigue pants, a very unconventional way of dressing judged Maria. What shocked Maria the most was that Tapa had a hunting knife in a leather case firmly attached to her right leg.

"Why do you carry a knife?" She asked Tapa.

“Tapa never know what she find in Chaco jungle?”

“Do you mean animals?”

“Animals with two legs! Men! “ exclaimed Tapa.

Maria Francisca Dominga was fascinated by Tapa and by the jungle they were crossing. Suddenly, a screeching noise broke the air.

“What’s that !” asked Maria with terror in her voice.

“Maria no afraid. Only noisy monkeys. Monkeys very beautiful! Them friendly. Monkeys no attack. If person annoy them, them attack.” said Tapa.

Maria terrified, hurried herself to be really close to Tapa.

“Maria, believe Tapa! No worry if Maria with Tapa. Maria worry about rich, drunk hunters. Maria keep away from them. Them come in jungle and shoot poor animals. Tapa see them shoot monkeys.”

“Hunting is a sport! explained Maria.

“Nice sport! No justice to kill for laughs” , Maria replied with a hint of anger in her voice. “Tapa tell you sad story. When Tapa child, Tapa see rich Senorito(7)shoot “she” monkey of

family. When macho monkey, see “she” monkey shot, he no escape. From tree, he look dead partner, then cried and cried until he also shot. Animals feel like Maria or Tapa”

Maria Francisca Dominga was embarrassed to tell Tapa that her father and her husband often went hunting. In an attempt to change the conversation she asked:

“How come that you were with them?”

“Papa work for them. Rich sloths! He was capataz(9), mama, brothers and sisters, and Tapa, all work for them. That day, them take Tapa to carry food and cook it. Tapa very upset because them kill for kill, and no kill for food because them are hungry. That day, Tapa promise to fight rich people."

They arrived at the river hot and puffing. The sun was quite strong despite the early hours. Maria marvelled at the variety of birds and their colours. She fall instantly in love with the toucans. Tapa knew all their names. She also knew the names of the trees and plants. Maria, deep in her thoughts, pondered about the emptiness of the world she had left. Her rigid attitudes, her beliefs, her prejudices horrified her. She wondered why she had never questioned them. Tapa in less than twenty four hours, had cast shadows in what she believed were unquestionable truths.

They undressed quickly. Maria could not keep her eyes from Tapa. She had no hairs on her body. A dark and curly mat grew between her legs. Her olive skin appeared smooth as silk. Her muscles were prominent, not only on her arms, but also on herlegs, her back, chest, and shoulders. She could not contain herself and asked how it was that she was so muscular.

"Maria have muscles too if Maria used as donkey. Tapa carry wood, water, dead animals, bags of flour! I was five when them, the masters, order Tapa to bring wood everyday into kitchen for the peones(10) to light them stove." The interest in each other's body was mutual, as Tapa gave a good look at Maria's body, thinking of how white and smooth her skin was.

"Maria too skinny!", she said as she held Maria's hand and ran with her towards the water. For a long time they swam in the warm waters of the river Bermejo. Then they sat under a tree to eat the fruits that Tapa had collected on their way there: wild berries, passion fruit, wild tiny apples and bananas.

They asked each other many questions. Tapa was a bit evasive about answering some questions and Maria lied in most of her answers. She told Tapa that her parents had died and that she came to Chaco hoping to get to know the Province, especially the jungle part. Maria did not lie about wanting to find a cheap place to live and work. The Indian woman offered to help. Tapa's cousin, with whom she lived had a spare room. She was sure that she was going to be most happy to rent it to her. She also knew people who could give her a job in a general store.

Maria Francisca Dominga could not make much sense of what Tapa's life was all about. She lived with her cousin in the town, a few kilometres away from the hotel. She was now at the hotel waiting for friends, who were coming to pick her upto go "training". When Maria tried to find out more about her friends, or the training, Tapa always changed the conversation.

Slowly they walked back to the hotel. Tapa was most concerned about Maria not getting hurt by the tree's branches that grew over the path, or with her tripping on the rough terrain. Maria had never had a friend so caring, in fact no*f*one had worried much about her. Like her children, she had been brought up by nannies and her parents never had much to do with her, except when they told her what she was not allowed to do. Maria Francisca Dominga was happy that she had met Tapa.

Tapa was well known in the little town, mainly by the shopkeepers, labourers and people who looked very poor. They went first to Tapa's cousin, Juana. When Maria arrived at the part of town where Juana's house it was, she immediately realised what sort of house was. She had seen neighbourhoods like this in other parts of Argentina, areas where poverty stricken people lived.

Maria had to make a great effort not to look shocked or upset by the poverty and misery of the place. The floor had no carpet, vinyl, nor even cement. It was simply a dirt floor. The house had three bedrooms. The one that she was going to rent was so small that it only accommodated a single bed and a side table. When Maria asked about a wardrobe, Tapa said that Juana would be most pleased to let her hang her clothes in her wardrobe.

Tapa spent a few minutes telling the story of the wardrobe, how beautiful and big it was, and how Juana was the first person in her family who owned one. She also was allowed to hang her clothes in Juana's wardrobe. Maria did not know if she felt like laughing or crying, the whole experience was so removed from her reality: a reality filled with the big and little things that money could buy.

Maria's thoughts went back to the wardrobes that she had owned during her life: the cute wardrobe that she had when she was a child, decorated with dolls and little flowers. The beautiful Queen Anne bedroom set that her parents had bought her for her fifteenth birthday and the dressing room, with built in wardrobes, mirror doors which her husband had asked the architect to design for her in the days before he had shown his real self.

"$10 pesos a week no much. I no ask you money until you get job. If you friend of Tapa you me friend too."

"Go on Maria, say Maria take it" , said Tapa encouragingly.

Maria was afraid to say yes. She was not sure if she was going to be able to live in this house with only one door,the front door, because each room had a curtain for a door. The windows had no glass or blinds only curtains as faded as the ones that hung over the doorsways, covered the tiny windows. The smell was also hard to take. It was not a smell of filth but a mouldy enclosed smell. With a tremor in her voice she said:

"I love to stay. Thank you Juana."

Walking to the general store, where Maria Francisca Dominga was going to ask for a job, gave her the chance to think about her having accepted the room. Why had she done it? She was not sure. She had the intuition that by living with Juana and Tapa she was going to learn about real life. But there was something else *f* Tapa. Tapa had made Maria curious. What was behind this woman? Why was she so intriguing? Why wasn't she rejecting her as her upbringing dictated?

"Hi Don Pedro! See this woman Maria, she finish school. She add, divide and multiply. Guara (12) answered Pedro's prays. She is the person Guara sent you."

"Experience?", asked the old man.

"Come on Don Pedro, you crazy? The lady no come to Pedro shop if she have experience?"

"I want someone smart, but also someone whom I don't have to teach everything", retorted Don Pedro.

"Big pity Don Pedro, because Don Jacinto want Maria. He pay $50 pesos a week, and $10 in groceries. Tapa said to Jacinto, we no interest because she work for me friend Don Pedro. O.K. Maria let's go. Some friends!"

"$40, I only can pay her $40, and I'll throw in some groceries."

"And... an ounce of tobacco a week", Tapa added.

"O.K.,O.K. Tapa, I know your ways, you'll pester me until I say yes. What happen to your friend? Can she speak for herself?"

It was obvious that Tapa knew how to make deals. Maria was to start the next day at 7 am . They were now going back to the hotel to pick up Maria's suitcase. Tapa had borrowed Don Pedro's truck and was driving towards the hotel.

"That was an impressive performance," said Maria.

"Performance?"

"Act, you acted like in the theatre."

"Well, life teach Tapa to fight for what she want", replied Tapa with a laugh. "What I don't understand is the tobacco? I don't smoke."

"I know, tobacco for an old , old Toba who live alone near river. Old man very poor and no*f*one care for old Toba. Maria will like him. He teach Tapa a lot. Maria lucky to give him the tobacco every week. Big honour!"

Maria again did not know what to say or think. Interacting with Tapa was sure an adventure in itself.

After collecting the suitcase Tapa was going to take her back to Juana's and then walk back to the hotel. Tapa's rendezvous with her friends was for the next day.

"When will you be back Tapa?" Maria asked as Tapa was getting in the truck.

"Tapa do not know. May be soon, may be not! While Tapa is away if you need help ask Juana. Juana help because I tell Juana to help. Guara bless Maria. Good luck with job! Ask Juana to take Maria to Don Ramon, and take tobacco. Tell Ramon you friend.

As Maria Francisca Dominga saw Tapa disappear from view, an intense feeling of loneliness invaded her. She walked into the house wanting to cry, but she couldn't. As she walked in, Juana led her to the small table where two plates had been set. A nice smell was coming from them.

"Guiso the Tripas(13)! Delicioso eh!" said Juana

Maria put the first mouthful of food in her mouth expecting to have to run to the outside toilet to vomit. People of her social class did not eat this sort of food. Maria did not vomit. She enjoyed the food very much, as well as the conversation. It was fascinating to hear Juana speak with the accent from a different province, with so many, varied and unusual expressions. Often she had to ask the meaning of some of the words. Some were in Quechua(14), some were very old fashioned Spanish words, and some were local idioms. Juana was uneducated but she was bright, but not as bright and smart as Tapa was.

After the meal, Maria asked where the toilet was. Juana pointed outside to a small tin construction at the back of the backyard. Under the black sky, adorned with millions of brilliant dots, she walked to the toilet. She was not surprised to find that the toilet had no electric lighting because the house had neither. A hole in the ground, barely visible, was all she found as a toilet! She smiled. She had never imagined that one day she was going to use this type of facility. On her way back, she rejoiced in the beautiful perfumes of the many tropical flowers that grew in Juana's rustic garden, and in those of the neighbouring houses.

Maria Francisca Dominga could not sleep. The sheets in the bed were rough and smelly, the mattress was made of straw and the mosquitoes were killing her. The events of the last few days flashed through her mind as if in a movie. She turned and tossed. She tried to pretend that she was back in Entre Rios in her comfortable bed. Juana snoring in the next room wasn't any help. She had not seen a shower in the house. How was she going to shower in the morning? She turned and tossed. Juana was now coughing. Remembering her children brought tears to her eyes. She sat up in bed and cried, begging the mosquitoes to leave her alone.

Juana's whistling woke her up. Maria found her in the kitchen trying to light the kerosene stove.

"Juana, where is the shower?", Maria inquired with a sleepy voice. Juana gave a hearty laugh and said:

"Good morning Tapa friend, my friend. If Maria Tapa friend, Maria know that no shower here. No*f*one shower here, only 'Capitalist bastards' as Tapa call them have shower. Where Maria come from? Come with Juana. Juana teach you how to wash." The Indian woman did not wait for the answer to her question, and shaking her head in disbelief, led Maria Francisca Dominga to the place where she was going to wash for the next few months. A tank, full of water, covered with a canvas over it, rested at the side of the house. The tank was hidden from the street by a wood panel and a few plants . Next to the tank there was a small bench with a big bucket, a small tin jug and a saucer with a piece of soap.

"Juana have to teach you how to wash too?", she asked in a sarcastic tone.

After washing and dressing, Maria ate the piece of dry bread and drank the big cup of mate cocido(15) that Juana had handed to her. Juana was not speaking as much as she had last night. She seemed a bit angry. She wished Maria good luck in her new job, pointing out how fortunate she was to get the job that so many of the town folks wanted.

Time at work went by very quickly. She learned many things and forced herself to be friendly to the clients. She had to force herself to be friendly because when she was upset she did not feel like talking to anyone. She avoided thinking about her children. To distract herself, she concentrated really hard in everything that she had to learn. Don Pedro taught her many things like weighing with an old fashioned scale, where things were and the price of the strange and numerous products. Don Pedro sold cotton to make clothes, foodstuffs, chicken feed, and seeds. He even had a catalogue from which people could order tractors and other heavy machinery.

At around two in the afternoon, Don Pedro gave Maria Francisca Dominga a sandwich of bread and cheese, and told her to go and rest for a while at the back of the shop. Maria did not want to rest. She wanted to keep busy in order to forget about her children. How crazy she had been abandoning them. She cursed herself and thought of taking her life. Was she a cruel and unnatural mother?

Late in the evening, Don Pedro sent her home with a loaf of bread, a small bag of garbanzos and half a dozen potatoes. When she got home she handed her small parcel to Juana. Juana was not angry any more. She was delighted with the groceries, and asked her to try to get some coffee, butter or perhaps some jam. These were very expensive luxuries. Maria Francisca Dominga felt embarrassed. Sshe had never imagined that some people in this world were deprived of many things. Had she been blind?

This time Juana had cooked a lentil stew with pig's trotters. Maria went over the same mental routine as the night before, wondering whether she was going to be sick with such unrefined food. She wasn't! She enjoyed very much every bit of the meal cooked by Tapa's cousin. After dinner Juana insisted that they play cards. There was still some daylight and, when the sun went down, she had an oil lamp that she lit on special occasions. Maria did not know how to play the games that Juana suggested, and Juana did not know to play canasta, bridge or poker. Besides Juana only had an old and greasy deck of Spanish cards.

Juana patiently taught Maria Francisca Dominga how to play Escoba de Quinces(15). After only a few practice runs, Maria was playing like an expert. During the game many times the conversation revolved around Tapa. Maria asked many questions about her, but many, especially those regarding what she was doing in the jungle, remained unanswered. It was obvious that Juana admired Tapa. Tapa was the only cousin in the family who was not a domestic.

Maria found out that Tapa bought and sold things for a living. Sometimes she picked up broken things from the rubbish bins of the rich people in town. Then she repaired and sold these things to the poor. Juana was quick to point out that Tapa never took advantage of anyone. She gave credit and many times, when people could not pay she forgot the debt.

Four weeks went by very quickly. During this time, she often thought about her children and even considered writing to them. She also realised that she was impatiently awaiting for Tapa's return. Was she going to tell her what she had been doing? Maria wanted to tell Tapa how thankful she was for helping her in the way she had. She also wanted to tell her that she took the tobacco to Don Ramon and that he was sick.

Last Sunday Maria and Juana had gone to take the tobacco to Don Ramon. They found him sick in bed. Maria was horrified at the poverty of the place Juana's place was a mansion compared with the shack where the old man lived. He had been in bed for a few days and had not seen a doctor, nor had he eaten anything. Immediately Juana started to clean the place up. Maria with apprehension helped her. After a while her nose had become accustomed to the bad smells. When they finished tidying up the place, they went to fetch the doctor, who promised to go to see the old man.

When Maria Francisca Dominga opened her eyes that Sunday morning, she saw Tapa sitting at the foot of her bed. She smiled and asked her how long she had been sitting there. Tapa had arrived an hour earlier and had not wanted to wake up Maria or Juana. She had sat very quietly observing Maria sleep. She had a surprise for her. Tapa insisted that she get up and come outside to see what she had bought. Maria, half sleep followed Tapa, who was dragging her outside by the hand. A big motorbike stood at the front door.

"Finally Tapa have motorbike. Tapa save for many months. A friend sell to Tapa. Friend know how much Tapa want the bike, friend wait for Tapa to save money." Maria was still sleepy. She hadn't yet got used to getting up early in the morning, but she commented on how beautiful and big the motorbike was, suggesting that one day they may go for a ride.

"Maria get ready! Tapa and Maria go for ride now, and swim too." Happiness glowed on her face.

Maria Francisca Dominga sat at the back of the motorbike. They were going swimming in the river Bermejo which flowed across the Chaco jungle. Maria Francisca Dominga put her arms around Tapa and rested her head on her big back. Tapa drove at high speeds over the dirt road. Maria's legs and arms were covered in dust, a dust that had attached itself to her hot and perspiring body. They parked the bike at the front patio of La Pantera Hotel and they walked across the jungle.

As once before, Tapa led the way. Again she was wearing green army pants and a knife tied to one of her legs. As they walked deeper into the jungle Tapa took her shirt off. A deep and wide wound ran across Tapa's back. With shock, Maria asked her what had happened to her. Tapa dismissed her wound as " Just a silly little cut." Maria promised herself that she was going to find out what Tapa was up to.

Naked they jumped into the river, they swam and played for hours in the water, racing and chasing each other. The water was cool and crystalline and many water birds rested on the river shore. Tired of the water, they laid down under the trees.

"Maria see that fat tree?" asked Tapa pointing at a tree with an unusual bulging trunk. Maria nodded and Tapa continued:

"The legend say that bad Spanish man rape beautiful Indian woman and left her with child. Indian woman no want child from bad man. Indian woman no want child with Spanish blood, the blood of the conquistadores. Moons pass and child big and big in belly. As child big and big Indian woman more and more desperate. She left Toba home and went to jungle. In jungle, for many moons Indian woman pray Guara for help. The day the moon was right for child to come into world, Guara come and say to Indian woman: "Guara give you wish, child never see world, and Indian woman live for ever. So Guara, very powerful, make Indian woman into that beautiful tree. See Maria, the pitaca(17) tree have shape of woman with child."

"That was a beautiful story", said Maria planting a kiss on Tapa's cheek. Tapa turned suddenly and holding Maria Francisca Dominga's face in her hands gave her a passionate kiss. Frightened by Maria's expression on her face she apologised:

"Tapa sorry. Tapa must no kiss you like man kiss woman. Tapa loss control. Tapa never again kiss Maria like this. Maria better know now what Tapa is. Tapa is tortillera(18).

Maria did not say anything. She got up and got dressed indicating her desire to return. Maria was confused. She should have slapped

Tapa for such action. She had done nothing to express her disapproval. But had she disapproved of Tapa's passionate kiss? While Tapa kissed her ,she had felt something that she had never experienced before. An intense sweetness had travelled across her body. How could it be? How could she feel such passion?... yes! it was passion that she had felt as Tapa had held her in her arms.

In silence, they walked back across the jungle towards where they had parked the motorbike. Maria engrossed in her thoughts led the way. She was trying to remember if her husband had kissed her like that before. No, he never had. Sometimes at the beginning of their relationship, when they first went out, he had kissed her gently. Later he became more and more brusque. Her wedding night was impregnated with bad memories. She had had her period. Iit had always came early when she was under stress. He did not care. He did not care either that she was a virgin. He had taken her without consideration, over and over while she had cried in silence.

With her friends, she had fantasized about romantic wedding nights and love making. How silly she had been! Never, in the years she had been married, had she enjoyed sex. Many times she had pretended to be asleep, hoping that he would leave her alone, but that had been of no help, as he had demanded his conjugal rights any time he wanted. One night, not long ago, he had forced her to have sex with him on the living room floor. He was drunk. Her screams had woken up her eldest child. He didn't care that the crying child was standing next to them. He raped her, finally falling asleep on top of her. She had pushed him off and with embarrassment and pain taken the child back to bed reassuring him that mummy and daddy were just playing.

The next day Maria went to speak to her mother. With embarrassment she related to her mother the brutality of his act. She begged her mother to allow her to come back home with the children. She couldn't endure the humiliations anylonger. Maria's mother refused to accept her in her home. She was married now and her place was with her husband and children. With a hint of sorrow in her voice she told her that it was her duty to serve her husband in any and every way he demanded. That was her duty as a "good Christian wife". That day Maria Francisca Dominga decided to leave her husband.

"Maria no move! Stop! Stop!!!" shouted Tapa with urgency in her voice. Maria stopped, realising that in front of her a big black snake was crossing at a leisurely pace. Maria froze, not a word came out of her mouth, and she trembled as the snake disappeared in the jungle.

"Better no disturb black snakes", said Tapa with sadness in her voice and eyes. Maria, looking into Tapa's eyes,crossed the distance that separated them:

"Oh Tapa!", she exclaimed as she hugged the Indian woman. Tapa extended her muscular arms and embraced her, covering Maria's face and neck with passionate kisses, murmuring comforting words in her ear. Maria, forgetting the nun's teachings, forgetting her rigid upbringing, and unable to control herself responded to Tapa's kisses with an unknown passion.

Maria Francisca Dominga returned Tapa's kisses. They kissed and kissed, their hands exploring each other's bodies.

"Let's go back to river", murmured Tapa. Holding hands they walked back to the river shore.

Tapa took off her clothes and helped Maria to take her dress. She pressed her warm and firm body against Maria's, caressing with her hands the back of the white woman. With gentleness she pushed Maria towards the sand. They lay on the beach cuddling and kissing. Sucking each other's nipples and tongues. Touching each other's legs and arms and bellies and breast. The intensity of the feelings prevented Maria from analysing them. She let herself melt in Tapa's passionate love making. They returned to Juana's place admiring the brilliant Southern Cross.

"Where Maria go? Juana sick worry about Maria not in bed. Tapa when you arrive? I know... I can see what Maria and Tapa do. Juana see red faces. I no care what Tapa do with woman, because Tapa is blood and good woman. I no like worries. I no like town people say Tapa tortillera. I worry no see Maria." "Sorry cousin, next time Tapa tell Juana we go swim", said Tapa hugging her angry cousin and telling her something in the Indian language, which Maria did not understand but which obviously made the woman forget her anger because both of them broke out laughing. Both Tapa and Juana laughed for a long time. Maria felt silly unable to understand the reason for their laugher.

That night the three of them ate the bean stew that Juana had prepared and sat under the moonlight in the backyard telling ghost stories and indian legends. Maria attentive listened to the fascinating tales that came out of the two beautiful Indian women. Suddenly Juana changed the conversation begging Tapa to tell stories about the CHE(19).

"Juana, Maria no want to hear about the CHE", said Tapa.

"Yes I do. But who is CHE?" Maria asked with curiosity.

"CHE great man! Come on Tapa tell us some of the stories you know," begged Juana.

"Che teaching Indians to read and fight rich pigs."

"Si! Si! CHE fight and give Indian their land back," exclaimed Juana with excitement.

"But who is he?" Maria inquired.

"Che is medicine man, but he only cure poor people and his soldiers. He very rich before, now poor like people he love. He loves America. He fight and make freedom for peasants, for Indians and poor people. He fight capitalists!" Tapa told many stories about this man and his teachings. Maria was fascinated by these ideas of freedom and revolution, ideas which if heard by her parents and husband would have made them mad. She smiled at the thought of them having to give away their land to the peasants they despised. Maria decided that she wanted to know more about this CHE and asked Maria where she could read about him.

"Next time Tapa see CHE, Tapa ask for books for Maria", she said with a very happy tone, obviously pleased that Maria was interested in her hero.

Maria and Juana had to get up early to go to work, so they decided to go to bed. Tapa sat outside for a long time. Before going to sleep she went to Maria's room to kiss her good night. As Tapa bent to kiss Maria, Maria, in a very soft voice said:

"I've been waiting for you. I missed you." Tapa, reading passion in Maria's eyes, kissed her while murmuring Quechua words in between kisses. They made love on the small single bed, their bodies illuminated by full moon. Exhausted they fall asleep in each other's arm.

The next day and for the following two weeks, Tapa drove Maria to her work and picked her up at closing time. Together they visited the old man, and Tapa paid the Doctor by repairing his old fridge. At night, they played cards with Juana, and they went for long walks, in the narrow streets of the small colonial town. During their walks Tapa spoke of her dreams. Tapa wanted the poor to have decent houses, schools and hospitals. She wanted them to share the richness of the country which was in the hands of a few "Terratenientes hijos de puta"(20).

Tapa also talked about her hero, the man who was going to liberate her country. Tapa told Maria that she trusted her so she wanted her to know about him and her companeros. Tapa was training to learn to fight. She was also learning to read. Now that Cuba was conquered Che wanted to free the rest of America. He wanted to start with Bolivia. She and her companeros were going to teach the people in all the Bolivian villages, then they were going to ask them to join in the fight against Capitalism.

"Maria remember wound on Tapa back? Wound from companero tonto, while training in jungle, nervous and insecure,"explained Tapa to Maria. In a few months, Tapa was going to join the Che in Bolivia. Guerrilleros (23) from all over South America would arrive the same day in the Bolivian sierras (24). Maria could not believe that Tapa was going to leave her, nor could she believe that she was going to fight.

As the days went by Maria grew sadder and sadder. A myriad of feelings had taken possession of her. She felt guilty because she belonged to the enemy: the rich. She felt distraught because she was going to lose Tapa. Tapa had told her that it was unlikely that she would return to Chaco. What was she going to do ? Continuing being a shop assistant? Vegetating in a small town? The guilt for having left her children had not abandoned her. Tapa had been so honest with her and she still had not told Tapa the truth about her past. How much she wished to have a dream like Tapa had! To know what she wanted out of life, to be prepared to die for your ideals.

As the weeks went by, Maria devoured the notes and books that Tapa brought her. Many nights, with Tapa and Juana, Maria spent hours discussing a view of the world which was new to her. Justice, freedom, equality, rights, they were all words which acquired a new meaning in her mind. One night, after making love in the tiny bed, with embarrassment she told Tapa about her past and background.

Tapa laughed at her. She was no fool. She knew all along that she was a Senora(25). She was very sorry about her children. Swearing her love for Maria and Che, Tapa promised her that one day, they were going to go back to Vera, and take the children away with them. Tapa declared that Maria's "guaguas"(20) were going to grow in the new America, a just world for everyone. That night Maria slept peacefully as she hadn't done in months.

"Tapa I want to go with you", Maria said, two weeks before Tapa's departure for Bolivia. Tapa had suspected that Maria may want to join the fighters. She had noticed how her interest and passion had grown as the weeks went by. Tapa wanted her to come, but Maria was not a fighter.

She tried to dissuade her. She explained to her that the life she had ahead was not an easy one. It involved sleeping outside, eating only when there was food available, hiding from the enemy, walking under the heat of the sun or under the tropical rain, being bitten by insects, being wounded and receiving only minimal medical attention, killing the enemy.

"... and if enemy catch you and not kill you, enemy torture Maria, enemy rape Maria until Maria talk, and Maria talk secrets. If enemy know secrets they kill more companeros. Maria lady, Maria wait home. Tapa promise, Tapa come back and pick Maria and then pick children," said the Indian woman. Tapa also told her that if she was going to join them there was no guarantee that they were going to be together. They may be ordered to be in different groups.

Maria did not care about any of the horrors that Tapa had painted for her. She wanted to be near Tapa, but also she wanted to fight for her new and strong ideals. She begged and cried. She cried and begged. Finally, Tapa agreed to take her for training so later she could join Tapa in the Bolivian' Sierras.

A few months later Maria joined Tapa. Maria's intelligence and physical fitness helped her to learn very quickly. She become a brave guerrillera and she won the admiration, not only of Tapa but of everyone in the group. Tapa and Maria never had many occasions for being on their own, but each minute that they shared together they treasured and valued. They were happy to know that they were close and that they were fighting for their dreams.

No one knows exactly when, but they say that on a rainy and humid morning Tapa and Maria Francisca Dominga died in combat with the enemy. Tapa was shot first. When Maria realised that Tapa had been shot, she ran between the crossfire to drag her to a safe place, but she was killed before she could reach her. Some compassionate Indians buried them together. The soldiers had kicked their faces to a pulp. They hated women fighters! They hated tortilleras!

Since their death, the Indian people of Chaco have a new legend to tell. In the little town of El Pintado, many people have seen two naked and beautiful women swim in the river Bermejo, a river that runs across the Chaco's jungle. Those who have seen them say that, one is short and dark: a strong Toba woman, and the other, a white blond European. When people go near them, their images disperse, as Chaco's hot sun shines through Maria's blond hair.

GLOSSARY

1. VERA

Small town in the Argentinian province Santa Fe.

2. CHACO

Province in the north of Argentina.

3. LA PANTERA

The Panther

4. TAPA

Lid

5. DOMINGA

Domingo:Sunday, as a female name: Dominga.

6. TOBA

Tobas,indians from Chaco.

7.SENORITO

The son of a distinguished person.

8.MACHO

Male animal.

9.CAPATAZ

Overseer, foreman.

10.PEONES

Labourers.

11.DON

Title for a gentleman.

11.GUARA(Quichua)

Mother of all spirits.

13.GUISO DE TRIPAS

Guts' stew.

14.QUECHUA OR QUICHUA

One of the languages spoken by South American'indians.

15.MATE COCIDO

Indian tea.

16.ESCOBA DE QUINCES

Spanish card game.

17. BITACA(Quichua)

South American tree shaped like a bottle.

18. TORTILLERA

Lesbian.

19. CHE

Ernesto Guevara (Che) (1928ƒ1967), Cuban revolutionary, born in Argentina. Died in Bolivia after capture for leaading communist guerrillas.

20.TERRATENIENTESƒ HIJOS DE PUTA

Land owners ƒ prostitute's sons.

21.COMPANEROS

Comrades.

22.TONTO

Silly.

23.GUERRILLEROS

Independent band of soldiers, engaged in guerrillas.

24.SIERRAS

Ridge of mountains.

25.SENORA

Lady.

26.GUAGUA(Quichua)

Small child.

www.ingramcontent.com/pod-product-compliance
Lightning Source LLC
Chambersburg PA
CBHW022200160726
48282CB00024B/266
9788119654192